Make Love Work for You

Make Love Work for You

An Essential Guide for
Career Couples

Julia Cole

Hodder & Stoughton
LONDON SYDNEY AUCKLAND

British Library Cataloguing in Publication Data
A record for this book is available from the British Library

ISBN 0 340 74595 9

Typeset by Avon Dataset Ltd, Bidford-on-Avon, Warks

Printed and bound in Great Britain by
The Guernsey Press Co. Ltd, Channel Isles

Hodder & Stoughton Ltd
A Division of Hodder Headline
338 Euston Road
London NW1 3BH

For my mother Barbara and stepfather Ralph

Contents

Acknowledgments   ix
Introduction   xi

1 **Balancing home and work life**   1
  Career couples in a new age   2
  What is your style?   8
  Life stages for career couples   16
  Chapter review   30

2 **Building your relationship when you both work**   31
  Before you meet   32
  Your new relationship   35
  Potential problems   38
  Learning from the early days   43
  Moving forward   50
  Chapter review   53

3 **Moving on – maintaining a successful working relationship**   54
  MOT your relationship   55
  Making adjustments   58
  Solving particular problems   67
  Differences in the way men and women look at problems   71

Common mid-term couple issues 77
Chapter review 81

4 Work, children and love – getting the balance right 82
Choosing children 83
Career couples during pregnancy 90
The growing child 96
Teenage children 104
About guilt 107
Chapter review 110

5 Keeping your love life alive when you both work 111
Common reasons for sexual problems 112
Common myths about sex 113
Improving your sex life 116
Practical help for love-making 128
Common sexual problems encountered by career couples 131
Chapter review 140

6 Problem busting – facing common concerns of career
couples 141
Managing family life when you both work 142
When you work together 149
Working from home 151
Holidays – pleasures or pains? 154
The career couple and infidelity 159
Managing social issues at work 166
Chapter review 170

7 Have you got a problem? Your most common questions
answered 171
Balancing home and work life 172
Building your relationship when you both work 174
Managing your life together as a career couple 177
The career couple and children 179
The career couple and sex 181
Career couples and common problems 183

Afterword 185
Further help 187
Index 193

Acknowledgments

I wish to express my thanks to all those who helped to make this book possible:

To Judith Longman of Hodder & Stoughton for her hard work and support in the genesis and completion of this book.

To Jo Frank, my agent, for her advice and help in all my writing.

To Adam and Hannah, my children, for all their patience and understanding.

To my husband Peter, without whom this book could not have been written.

Introduction

Do you feel overwhelmed by juggling your relationship, work and family? Do you sometimes find it hard to choose – work or partner? Do you sometimes argue about who should wash up or cook the evening meal? If so, this is the book for you.

This book is about how to balance home and work life and come out on top. For many couples, this is the issue that takes up hours of discussion and often prompts arguments. From deciding how bills will be paid when you first move in together to handling the conflicting demands of a partner who wants to spend time with you when you should be finishing paperwork and coping with the demands of family life as you deal with your finances, couples everywhere are learning how to be working couples.

This is a brand new issue for the Millennium generation. No generation before this one has had men and women working as equals, both with the right to be at work and both asking for exactly the same respect as each other. This revolution demands new approaches to relationships and work that allows couples to feel secure and safe in their partnerships whilst working to their best standard.

But this is not an easy thing to achieve. Many couples find themselves bogged down in the minutiae of everyday life. They may feel frustrated at the repeated rows over housework and childcare or wish they felt interested in sex more often and less tired.

Make Love Work for You offers practical ideas on managing these issues and more. The book begins with an explanation of why couples are facing change in their relationships and moves on to offer help in building a relationship when you both work. Chapter Two helps you to understand the common assumptions made by couples and how to deal with these, offering help in understanding the different approaches of men and women to problem solving. Chapter Four looks at children and their impact on the working couple, giving practical advice on deciding to have children as well as help in deciding about childcare and the division of parenting. Chapter Five offers advice on how to keep the intimate side of your partnership alive, offering help on dealing with loss of sex drive through tiredness and stress. Chapter Six will help you to beat those problems that can assail the career couple, such as how to work together successfully, have a good holiday and learn to work from home. The book concludes with a selection of questions from couples coping with career and relationship issues, each with an individual answer on the subject for which they are seeking help.

My hope is that this book will inspire you to tackle your relationship and make love work for you. You could have a relationship that is in perfect balance just waiting for you to discover, so start reading now!

1

Balancing home
and work life

This book is about the most important issue that a great many modern couples face – how to balance the demands of home and work. This means more than 'just surviving' as a couple or parents. Creating a balance means that work, home and leisure can each receive the attention they deserve. If work dominates your life so that your family never sees you, or home life is so stressful that your work suffers, you have lost the balance that can make all the difference between a life worth living and a life that feels like a constant slog. The question, 'Do you work to live or live to work?' has never been more relevant.

Currently four in ten of all marriages are predicted to end in divorce. This represents a trebling in divorce in the UK since 1969. Fifty-six per cent of divorces affect children under the age of 16. The need to create relationships that are secure and long lasting is seen as important not only to individuals, but also society at large.

Many reports indicate that stable relationships help people to enjoy life and work more effectively. (Divorced and separated people are likely to drink and smoke more heavily, as well as to suffer from depression.) In other words, if you can get the home/work balance right, you can have a partnership that is fulfilling and a life that is fun as well as satisfying, without running the risk that you will end up as a divorce statistic or coping with a broken commitment. This book will show you how to achieve a healthy balance in your home and work life.

Career couples in a new age

So why is it that, as we enter a new Millennium, so many couples are struggling to get this crucial balance right? As a couple counsellor, I often meet people who say that their inability to cope with the demands of home and work has all but destroyed their relationship. Frequently, one partner feels that the other works too hard, does not work hard enough, does too much housework or does not help with the housework at all. Arguments over childcare, money or sex seem to occur with monotonous regularity. Despite the fact that many people enjoy a more affluent lifestyle, often with both partners working in full-time jobs, with luxuries such as a car, TV or washing machine – all inventions that would have amazed their grandparents and great-grandparents – many couples still report feeling exhausted by their lifestyles rather than freed to enjoy their leisure time.

Perhaps part of the answer to this question lies in the history of relationships and work. Until recently, not only were women less likely to work in paid employment, but if they did work, their work was less valued than that of a man. Women have, historically speaking, been less likely to earn the same wages as men and have often been denied the chance of an education and career. One hundred years ago the middle classes still had servants (often poorly paid women) to help with housework. Women in the middle and upper classes were not expected to work or follow a career. Female teachers, for instance, were not allowed to teach if they married because it was assumed they would need to leave in order to care for their husbands. Poorer people were expected to work extremely hard to earn very little. Women in these social groupings often took in washing or undertook repetitive work in factories. Even where women worked in better jobs, their contribution was often viewed as sub-standard in comparison to men. The notion that a man and woman could both follow a professional career or have jobs that paid equal money to both sexes would have astounded men and women in the late 1890s and 1900s. But all this began to change after the First World War and, to a greater extent, during and after the Second World War. With men called away to fight, women were brought into the limelight, often undertaking jobs that would have been almost exclusively male only a few weeks before. Women worked in factories, docks and offices, proving that women could do all the same things as a man. When the wars ended, women were expected to return to their homes – cooking and cleaning for the men so recently back from fighting. But by the 1950s women had glimpsed another life. Many of the advertising images of the time show the pipe-smoking husband being served by a smiling woman. New technologies, such as electric cookers, were commonly advertised with women cooking and looking radiant in a modern kitchen. The message to women seems to have been 'get back in the kitchen'! Men were rarely shown in this environment, being more likely to be seen listening to the radio whilst awaiting an evening meal. In short, women were asked to give up their new-found work skills so that men could return to the jobs and education abandoned when they were called up into the Armed Forces. To be fair, many women appeared to accept this situation. But it is possible to trace the roots of feminism to this enforced change. Women began to ask themselves, 'If I (or my mother) could do the same kinds of things as a man, why must I accept a life based only at home?' And so began the notion that women had the right to be accepted as valid in the work-force and not to be seen only in the role of nurturer to children. Of course, the role of motherhood is still extremely important to many women, and most women gain a sense of positive self-esteem from caring for their children, but modern women would probably balk at being defined only in terms of motherhood.

Since the 1960s women have seized the opportunity to attend further education, follow careers and hold down a job. Recent statistics suggest that 37 per cent of mothers aged 25 to 34 return to work within a year of the birth of their first child compared to only 14 per cent of mothers now aged 60 to 64. Both parents are now much more likely to have jobs. In 1995, 62 per cent of married couples of working age with children were in paid work. This represents an increase of 12 per cent since 1985. Most people would probably agree that this is a good thing. Women *should* have the right to be the equal of men. This does not always mean that women want to do exactly the same kind of work as men, but that they should be accorded the same respect for the work they do undertake. But this seismic change in the way that men and women work has caused a tidal wave of change in the way that they relate to each other. Until the 1960s most people in the UK still held neat stereo-types of how men and women should behave in a marriage. (Marriage was still the accepted way of conducting a couple relation-ship – cohabiting did not really become popular until the late 1970s.) Men were expected to be the 'breadwinners' and women the 'home-makers'. If women worked they were expected to undertake work that fitted around the role of the man, rather than vice versa. Women who worked while their children were small often invited censure. Those who did work often did so from economic necessity, rather than as a lifestyle choice, and there was little support for them in society at large. Childcare was often undertaken by relatives or friends and largely unregulated.

A survey taken in 1955 found that couples said the most import-ant thing in marriage was 'fulfilling the roles of breadwinner and homemaker'. By 1970, when the same survey was repeated with a new set of couples, the finding was that the 'most important thing was that husbands and wives liked each other'. Couples had moved from seeing couple relationships as fixed roles to seeing them as private relationships that were more about individual similarities and differences than a particular set way of behaving. Although this was freeing, it also brought different responsibilities. For men, all the change that had taken place in the role of women meant that they were expected to play a continual 'catching up' game. As women asked for greater equality, men had to come to terms with what the changes meant for them. From an assumption, at the turn of the century, that men were better equipped to work and to lead women, men found themselves fifty years later being asked to accept women as complete equals in fields that had been previously denied to them. Women also began to ask men to change their attitudes to what had been traditionally called 'women's work' – domestic chores and childrearing. With more women working, men were expected to help with washing up and bathing the baby rather than sitting down to read the paper after a day at work. Men were increasingly seen as partners in childcare rather than passive observers. For instance, in the late 1960s and early 1970s men were admitted to the labour ward and asked to support their partner during birth. Some men resisted this (indeed, some men still do resist the idea that they should share domestic tasks, insisting that they are the role of the woman alone). But most men tried to fulfil the new role that was asked of them. Some of them reported that this experience felt confusing and strange. Others felt embarrassed at undertaking chores that their fathers would have never considered suitable for a man to do – such as changing a nappy. Men tended to describe this activity as 'helping my wife', rather than seeing it as a valid nurturing role for themselves as a father. But as the 70s and 80s went on, men were expected to become 'new men'. The 'new man' was not only expected to take on a more active role in the home, nurturing the children and sharing routine daily tasks, but also to be more in touch with his feelings and emotions. Women also often gave a mixed message to the men in their lives – 'be sensitive, but be macho as well'. It is no surprise that the call to a return to 'family values' occurred in the mid-1980s. Men and women found themselves struggling with what it meant to be in a couple relationship. The neat stereotype of 'dad at work and mum at home' had gone for ever. In its place was a confusing tangle of feelings and contradictory demands that often meant that couples did not know where to start in creating a practical partnership for the future. The call for 'family values' was really a desire to turn the clock back to a time when men and women knew what was expected of them, however constricting this was for both sexes. Sometimes, the comfort of the known and understood can seem more attractive than the new and strange, even when the new thing promises to be worth exploring.

So what about today? Relationships are changing. More and more couples are choosing to cohabit rather than get married. The Government Actuary's department has forecast that the proportion of the adult population in England and Wales who are married will drop from 55 per cent in 1996 to 45 per cent in 2021. The number of cohabiting couples, estimated to be 1.56 million in 1996, will double over the next twenty-five years. The proportion of births outside marriage has risen steeply over the last twenty-five years. In 1996 they accounted for just over a third of births, more than four times the proportion in 1971. Couples are choosing to be together for different reasons – some know they want to make a short-term partnership, others only marry when they want a family, while others never marry but still want to be parents. Gay couples and single people can now adopt and foster children. When we say 'family' it can now mean a multiplicity of experiences – some shared and some unique. This means that couples have to 'reinvent the wheel' for themselves.

Without a stock pattern of behaviour to follow, the successful career couple have to devise a way of communicating and working together that covers all the changes they may encounter, as well as day-to-day living. It is this that has proved tricky for many couples. Finding a way of talking about difficult issues, such as sex, money and childcare, can be a minefield. Here are some of the most common difficulties that many couples discover when they talk about the kind of relationship they want:

- **Assumptions**
  It is easy to make assumptions about what your partner may be looking for from your relationship. When the partnership begins, you may see in-depth discussions as unromantic and never voice your views about work or children. As the relationship deepens, it

is easy to assume that you and your partner see things in the same light. When you eventually get round to talking about tricky subjects it can be a shock suddenly to discover that he does not want children or that she intends to carry on her career, even though you have a new baby, when you had assumed that the opposite would happen.

- **Expectations**
  Although expectations are similar to assumptions, they are more concerned with what both partners want and hope for from the relationship. For instance, Rose expected that her boyfriend would divide his salary in such a way that he would make an equal contribution to the rent. He felt that the relationship was likely to be short-lived and so decided that he would not share his cash in the way Rose expected. The result was a series of arguments that ultimately ended the relationship. Unshared expectations can be a cause of disagreement once the relationship begins to mature. This can often happen if one partner shields their true expectations from the other instead of being honest about what they expect.

- **Beliefs about the role their partner should play**
  Different beliefs can affect the way in which people develop a view of how their partner should behave. Many couples come from families of origin that are very different in their approach to relationships. For example, you may come from a family that is very open. Every subject is up for grabs and talked about openly. You may be used to hearing your parents, brothers and sisters talking about money or politics over the kitchen table. Your partner may have come from a family where just the opposite happened. They may have experienced tightly controlled conversations, with taboo subjects that must not be broached. These family experiences can cause problems when a couple try to communicate; they may believe a partner should be open or discreet because that is what they learnt from observing their parents. Some religious and ethnic backgrounds may also predispose

people to believe that a partner should behave in a particular way and cause dissent when the belief is opposed. For example, some cultures believe it is wrong for a woman to work or for a man to care for children.

- *Particular ideas about how a couple should operate*
You may find that hidden beneath your general expectations of how you expect your partner to behave are more specific attitudes towards what should happen in your partnership. For instance, you may privately believe that men should always initiate sex, or that women should take on the brunt of the housework. This can handicap you when discussing issues that require a resolution – such as who should ask for love-making or which partner should clean the bathroom! This is because you may find yourself unable to change your view or simply leave your personal bias out of the conversation. It is important to be self-aware when discussing any relationship issue, because your attitudes could significantly influence the outcome.

What is your style?

All these ways of thinking and behaving come from a particular set of values and ideas learnt over the years. Some will have come from your parents, others from your friends, personal culture, ethnic background, the media and many other areas of influence. Use the following questionnaire to help you decide where your ideas about work and relationships come from. Tick the answer which is nearest to your situation and note which of the four options (a, b, c, or d) you choose most frequently. When you have finished, read the most relevant section to help you understand how you formulated your ideas about managing home and work life.

Q1
We have mostly based our relationship on:

a) Our parents, and the way they conduct their partnerships.
b) Our own decisions and deliberations.
c) Observing what works for our friends.
d) All of the above options together.

Q2
When one or both of us is thinking about starting or changing a job, we:

a) Follow the pattern of our families as far as possible, or ask our family for advice.
b) Talk about the options open to us and make decisions based on the best one.
c) Ask our friends for their opinions, as these are as important to us as our personal decisions.
d) Try to take an overview of all the different ideas to help us decide what to do.

Q3
If we disagree about an aspect of home or work life – too much time spent at work, for instance – we:

a) Confide in our family, asking how they would solve the problem.
b) Confront the issue, even if it means arguing about the problem.
c) Try to discover if other friends had shared the same experience.
d) Seek other forms of help to intercede in the problem.

Q4
When planning an aspect of home life that requires team work – such as deciding who should use the car to get to work on certain days – we:

a) Use our families as a model, even if one of the partners is

disadvantaged by this situation.
b) Decide each day, according to our needs for the day.
c) See if friends agree with one partner or another.
d) Ask others for their view.

Q5
We tend to arrange our finances:

a) In a similar style to our parents or family – using the same bank or building society, for example.
b) To suit ourselves and according to our circumstances at the time.
c) In a similar way to friends or others we admire. For instance, we may decide to buy a particular item because a friend has the same one.
d) We read or ask for all the available information before making a decision. For example, we may tour all the local garages for months comparing models and prices before buying a car.

Q6
When making decisions about work or home we:

a) Are fairly cautious and stick to proven solutions.
b) Sometimes take risks, but enjoy the chance of finding a new way to do things.
c) Often choose the modern or latest way to do things.
d) Spend a long time thinking about what to do.

Q7
We share most household tasks:

a) True, but the woman does most of the household activities while the man undertakes other chores.
b) Yes, but not in a planned way.
c) Sometimes, but it can be a source of tension.
d) Yes, and we have a clear plan of who does what.

Q8
If we have children, we talk about their care:

a) Sometimes, but we do not need to have in-depth conversations because we have a daily routine that works.
b) Yes, usually as each concern comes to the surface.
c) Sometimes, but we can feel unsure of how to proceed.
d) Yes, but we often use books or magazines to help us decide what to do.

Q9
When we argue over work or home the issues are often concerned with:

a) One partner feeling put upon by the other.
b) Forgotten tasks or promises.
c) A problem over who does what around the house or at work.
d) Decisions that take too long to agree.

Q10
We are satisfied with your style of balancing home and work:

a) Most of the time, but we would sometimes like greater variation.
b) Yes, but sometimes it feels erratic and confused.
c) Yes, but occasionally it feels as if we follow fashion rather than what pleases us.
d) Some of the time, but we can feel it is too much of a chore.

Mostly As

You are a fairly traditional couple who tend to look to parents and family tradition for insight into conducting your partnership. You may have strong cultural or ethnic reasons for feeling that your families of origin have the best pattern for relationships – for example, you may both be Jewish or Muslim – or have been strongly impressed by your family style of relating to each other for other reasons. This may be due to a conservative and carefully considered relationship style, or simply that you admire your parents' way of living and want to copy it, indicating that you had a very happy family life. Alternatively, it could mean that your parents were rigid in their attitude to managing family life and left you with little knowledge or experience of alternative choices. You may sometimes feel constrained to, or repressed in, a certain role within the relationship, which can be frustrating at times. If you do not experience these feelings, you may feel satisfied with the relationship because it works well for you at the moment. Problems may emerge if one of you desires change – perhaps because one partner wants to take up a new job or becomes ill.

Here are some ways to manage change in an 'A' type relationship that minimise possible difficulties.

- Try to make an assessment about whether the way your family does things *is* right for you. Look carefully at your individual circumstances. For instance, Ruth felt that it was right that her husband, Phil, should work full time to support the family because her father had always done the same. Phil wanted to take time off to do a part-time degree, and asked Ruth to look for a part-time job. Ruth was angry and upset, failing to understand the differences between their situation and that of her family. Lack of adaptability in relationships can result in one or both partners feeling trapped.

- If you want to follow certain traditions because your culture and background demand it, you also need to talk to one another about your feelings and expectations of your personal relationship. It is easy to make an assumption about what your partner is feeling because you think you know how a man or a woman should feel in your particular culture. Respecting your partner as an individual is still important even if you do follow a prescribed style of relating.

- Some A-type couples develop a 'blinkered' approach to their relationships, screening out other ways of relating – perhaps through anxiety about making decisions about the future that do not follow a well-known route. Try taking a sample situation that you can discuss, preferably one that you have not already encountered, and talk about how you would handle it. This kind of rehearsing is a safe way to explore different methods of managing your relationship.

Use the following examples to get you started, or any others that are pertinent to you.

1. You both get the chance to move house to a new and unknown area. Should you take the opportunity?
2. One of you is left a legacy of £30,000. How will you use it?
3. One of you becomes seriously ill and unable to work or manage the family. How will you cope?

Mostly Bs

You are a fiercely independent couple who nearly always follow a highly individual path in your relationship and take little notice of tradition or the style of your family of origin. You probably have a good pattern of communication, although it can sometimes result in arguments and a sense of confusion before you resolve issues. Occasionally, one or both of you may long for a less idiosyncratic approach to your partnership and look for a simple solution to problems. You are innovative and often find new ways of doing things, so that your relationship is usually exciting and fizzing with life. Other people may find you slightly daunting because it may be hard to discover a point of reference with you, but you are hardly ever concerned about the opinions of others.

Here are some issues for people in B-type relationships to consider:

• Do you sometimes 'throw the baby out with the bath water'? In other words, do you sometimes reject a way of relating simply because it is the accepted way, rather than considering it on its own merits? For example, Lucy and Samuel decided they would not marry because they came from families where marriage was the expected path of a couple in a close relationship. Neither considered whether marriage had any merit, but chose to cohabit

because it was different from their family backgrounds.
- You can still be independent while creating routines that help to smooth family life. Arranging a rota or agreeing certain basic principles to support the foundations of your relationship can help you to feel less confused and more able to manage any change that occurs.
- Ask yourself if you are trying to avoid traditional patterns of life because you are running away from something painful or difficult in your past. For instance, you may decide to behave differently in a second relationship because of an emotional hurt from your first relationship. It may be that you could retain some of the good things from a previous relationship without endangering the present one.

Mostly Cs

You are a couple who usually feel nervous about taking decisions based on your own beliefs or ideas. You often seek the approval of others, usually friends rather than family. You want to keep up with modern ideas about being in a couple or raising children; this can be helpful, but only if you are not constantly changing your stance in order to follow fashion. You may be willing to seek advice from others, but this has the hidden danger of swaying you from one idea to another so that you can feel confused by all the different opinions available to you. You may find it frustrating to feel part of a group of friends or associates who all live similar lifestyles, rather than having a relationship that allows you to be creative about what *you* want from your partnership. You can feel split by the opposite opinions of friends, and this can cause arguments.

For instance, Rosemary asked her friend Kate for her opinion about returning to work after the birth of her daughter. Her partner Paul asked his friend Keith about whether his partner had returned to work after the birth of their child. Kate told Rosemary that she felt it was a good thing, whereas Keith felt it was not helpful, chiefly because their child had developed sleeping problems that had put them under a great deal of stress. Rosemary and Paul argued over

Rosemary's return to work, rather than considering what would suit them as individuals and as a couple.

Here are some suggestions for building a more independent C-type relationship:

- Take the risk of believing in your own hopes and ideas occasionally. Ask your partner what they want and make a practice of stating your own expectations more often. Agree to ban all sentences that begin 'My friend (name) says . . .'
- Make a list of all the things you would like to try that you have not done. For instance, you may always choose the trendiest holiday destination rather than go to the place you would like to explore. Pick the ones on the list that are achievable and agree to try them in the coming months.
- Break out of your normal routine and try a different way of relating. If you always spend Saturday nights with friends, try going out for an evening on your own. Do not always discuss personal issues with friends. Instead, talk to each other about what *you* want and try to put it into practice. There is nothing intrinsically wrong with talking to friends about some aspects of your relationship, but remember to protect important aspects of your life together. Discussing sex and money with friends may seem tempting but can often cause your partner to feel betrayed rather than supported, especially if you have developed problems in this area.

Mostly Ds

You are a couple who reflect a great deal on what you want from your relationship. This can be positive, because you probably pay a lot of attention to the views of your partner and what will be right for your partnership. But it may also mean that you are very cautious about decision-making and this can sometimes lead to a stalemate over particular concerns. You may want to take some risks, but fear the problems which may result if you do not give a lot of care and attention to your relationship and any joint decisions you make.

Although you are usually good at talking through issues, you may take so long to reach a conclusion that you lose the momentum needed to take action. You are usually good at planning and able to see difficulties around the corner. This attribute means that you often avoid problems, but it can also mean that you do not enjoy surprises and lack spontaneity in everyday life.

Here are some ideas to improve D-type relationships:

- It is right that you are concerned for your partner, but you might agree a pact where one of you chooses all the activities on a given day. For example, you could agree to have a day out together but leave all the arrangements to one partner alone, to choose something they would particularly enjoy, with the other partner's desires coming second.
- Listen to your instincts more than you do at the moment. Personal intuition is often underrated and can make a valuable contribution to relationships. Try out intuition during your next weekly shopping trip; buy items you would like to try as well as those that are best value or that you know your partner likes. You may spend a little more occasionally, but you could enjoy the new experience.
- Break your usual routine sometimes. For instance, if one partner always cooks, swap roles once or twice a week. Taking practical action in this way can help to break your sometimes constricting and long-winded thought processes.

Life stages for career couples

Understanding the type of relationship you are in can help you to make sense of how you approach relationships in general, and also how you decide what to prioritise in balancing your work and home life. You may find that your relationship works well in daily life, but can encounter difficulties during times of change. Use your knowledge about your relationships, gained from the questionnaire, to consider how you might approach the following concerns; all of them are common life-changing events and you are likely to encounter at least some of them. To help you make sense of them, each stage has a case study for you to compare with your own approach.

Deciding to move into a long-term relationship after a more casual relationship

You may not be aware that you are moving into a deeper relationship, or may quickly realise that the person you have been seeing is special and that you are likely to be together for some time. Although you may not realise it, during this period you are unconsciously setting up how you will manage your relationship in the future. It can be helpful to express your expectations, especially if you are aware that your partner has particular views about work or the roles you will take up if you stay together.

Case Study
Heather and Will met during a swimming gala at their local leisure centre. They were immediately attracted and were inseparable for several months. Heather liked Will because he shared her sporting interests and they often played badminton or tennis together. Will thought that Heather was a 'tough cookie' – practical and assertive – which he found attractive and exciting. He made an assumption that Heather would want to pursue her career as a PE teacher in the future and went on believing this when they eventually moved in together. But Heather had a private dream: she wanted to become an independent sports adviser. This was not without risks. It meant giving up a safe salaried position to take on freelance work, but once she and Will were living together she reasoned she could seize the opportunity to branch out. When she told Will she had given in her notice he was completely taken by surprise. All his assumptions about the future were thrown into disarray and they went through a difficult time, arguing and enduring long silences, before Will realised that the attributes he most admired about Heather were precisely the things that made her want to try a new style of work.

* * *

17

As with Will and Heather, it is useful to check out assumptions and private ideas about how the relationship will proceed rather than decide independently that things will stay the same in the future. Some couples are afraid to tackle this, because it can seem hard to talk about change when only just beginning a relationship. If you recognise yourself in this description, try to see the sharing of hopes and dreams for the future as part of the building of the partnership rather than spoiling the pleasure of the moment. You may decide not to talk about the future too prematurely, especially if you are unsure about the long-term future of the relationship. This is OK for a few months, but once you know the partnership is growing and maturing, take time to look into the future. You may not stick faithfully to your plans, but it will help you to plan more effectively when you do need to make some decisions.

Deciding how to live together

Once you have taken the step to choose to live together, whether you have decided to marry or cohabit, you need to think about who does what around the home you share. The truth is that most relationships stand or fall, not by the excitement of the sex, but by which partner does the washing up! Never allow certain routines to develop by default. For instance, you may enjoy cooking and be pleased to do it for a few weeks in the first flush of romance, especially if your partner says how great it is. But after a few months you will feel resentful if your partner flops down in front of the TV while you are stuck in the kitchen – again – after a hard day at work.

Case Study

Alice and Marc met at university and married soon after leaving. They had not lived together beforehand but soon began to enjoy setting up home together. Both had been fortunate enough to find reasonably well-paid jobs – Alice in the media industry and Marc in a local pharmaceutical firm. As they were just starting, both were keen to impress their superiors and therefore often worked longer hours than were strictly necessary. Soon their home filled up with a muddle of newspapers and used coffee cups. Alice blamed Marc for laziness, while Marc told Alice she was 'useless at housework'. After some months of bickering, they decided to sit down and try to sort things out. Alice explained that her father had done a great deal of the housework because her mother was a nurse and often on long shifts, which prevented her from doing much in the house. Marc responded by saying that his mother had taken a traditional role in the home, carrying out most of the household tasks. Both quickly saw that, because of their family experiences, each of them had expected the other to deal with the daily chores. Together they drew up a list of tasks and divided them between them. This solved their problems and stopped rows overnight – except occasionally when Alice forgot to clean the bathroom or Marc felt too tired to cook!

At the start of most long-term relationships, both partners are adjusting to a way of being with another person that is completely new. Even if they have had a hundred relationships prior to the one they are embarking on, the new relationship is unique. This can be at once both exciting and emotionally tiring. Add to this the everyday chores that every couple encounters and you may feel tired rather than full of life – especially if you have moved house to a strange environment. Give yourself time to adjust to this new life, adding in time for relaxation and fun as well as painting and decorating! This is the time when you can bond with each other in a deep way. Simple things like sharing a take-away meal, walking in the park, watching a video together and enjoying love-making, can all help you to manage the 'under development' early stage of being together.

Thinking about a family

Not every couple wants to have a child. In fact, the birth rate is dropping dramatically in Europe, so it may be that more couples are deciding to remain childless than ever before. But discussing whether you want to become parents is an important part of early-stage relationships. It not only has a crucial influence on your intimate relationship, but also on your decision-making process about work.

If you both decide to carry on working, you will have to find childcare that you are happy about. If one of you stops work, you must take a long hard look at your financial situation and make a realistic assessment about how you can afford to care for a child. This topic seems to cause many couples a great deal of difficulty. They may feel that they should have children, but do not really want to, or want children but feel they cannot afford them. Others seem to put the whole issue in the lap of the gods, hoping that an accidental pregnancy will take the decision away. Of all the options available, this is the one that can be fraught with problems – including the resentment of the partner who was not consulted. It is also unfair to use a child to make a decision that the adults involved should have taken by themselves.

Case Study

Noel and Sally had been married for eighteen months when they began to discuss seriously whether they should start a family. They had lived together prior to marriage for a number of years and had married partly because they wanted to start a family. But shortly after they married Sally was offered promotion at her job. She had not expected this, but accepted her new role with great pleasure. Noel and Sally had postponed their plans to become parents so that Sally could settle into her new position at work. Noel wanted to be a father but put his hopes on hold for Sally's sake. But as time passed, he began to ask her about starting a family. At eighteen months, they knew they had to make a decision. Sally felt torn because she wanted to remain in her career and try for further promotion, but she also wanted to become a mother. They spent several weeks discussing the issues, finding it harder and harder to find a solution. Eventually, Sally spoke to her Personnel Director about her dilemma. He helped her to look at career options that allowed for her and Noel starting a family. After further discussions with Noel, they began to try for a baby and Sally became pregnant five months later.

When thinking about having a baby, you need to consider the long-term impact on your circumstances. Sally and Noel thought through all the options open to them. This enabled them to arrive at a conclusion that was satisfactory for them. If Noel had been less understanding about Sally's career, or Sally had avoided talking to Noel about her plans for the future, the relationship could have run into serious difficulties. If you want to talk about having a child (or not having children), try to give yourself time to think through the issues. For instance, you might ask yourself some important questions, such as 'Why do we want a baby? Why do we want a baby *now*?', and 'What changes would we need to make if we start a family?' This kind of talking is a process. Do not hope to come up with all the answers in a half-hour conversation over your morning coffee. You may also find that you shift your position on particular concerns – for example, you may have always intended returning to work only to feel this is not tenable. This is natural as you take such an important decision. You will probably find that you settle for one course of action after a while.

This issue can also raise strong disagreements. Usually, these kinds of arguments stem from the inflexibility of one partner or the other. For instance, the woman may wish to stay at home with the baby while her partner demands that she returns to work for the sake of their finances. Increasingly, rows can occur at the stage of deciding to have a family because many couples now have a variety of choices. Modern couples may find this area difficult to deal with because they face so many choices about how to conduct their relationships. The stereotypical picture of the woman at home with the children has been swept away. This means that each couple has to make a complex set of decisions about when to have a child, who will care for it and how to support the growing family. If a partner is inflexible in his or her approach, this can prevent both partners from looking at the choices open to them. It can help to list all the possible choices. The list can then be whittled down to the most appropriate decisions. For instance, a couple may decide that they want to delay thinking about a family because the list shows that their financial situation is not stable, or they may decide to start a family in order to have a child before they take on a great deal of responsibility in their chosen work. Of course, many couples make the decision to have a child quickly, easily and with little discussion. But for many couples, it is an issue that requires a great deal of thinking through. There is more about choosing to have a child and managing childcare in Chapter Four.

Coping with small children

This phase of couple relationships is perhaps the most difficult for the working couple. Small children are totally dependent on their parents for care and attention. This is obviously not only physical but also emotional care. If both parents work, or even if just one is in paid work, the amount of energy and commitment required to care for small children can be extremely draining. Deciding who will do what, and when, for the child can be a stumbling block for parents, especially if they have not discussed beforehand how childcare should be shared. You can read more in Chapter Four on how to manage childcare concerns, but many couples do have to work hard to maintain their relationship after the birth of a child. In fact, most divorces occur five to nine years after the wedding – a time when many couples are starting a family or have small children to care for.

Case Study

Lucas and Clare had been married three years when they had their first child, a daughter named Isabel. Lucas was a freelance garden designer, while Clare worked in a local bank. Although they did talk through who would care for Isabel when Clare returned to work, neither was fully prepared for the impact of a small baby on their chosen careers. Clare had very little sleep during her maternity leave and found returning to work extremely hard. Lucas had agreed to care for Isabel at least part of the day, but found that she interfered with his ability to work in an '*ad hoc*' way, often determined by the weather because he was out of doors most of the time. After discussion with Lucas, Clare agreed to cut her hours at the bank, working part time instead of full time. But this had a severe impact on their income and Clare began to feel depressed by their lack of cash. She and Lucas argued because Clare thought that Lucas should

22

have been able to integrate care for Isabel into his day, while Lucas felt that Clare did not understand the real nature of his work. For several months, their relationship was tense and difficult. Eventually Clare decided to look for a child-minder, but encountered problems with this course of action because her mother thought that Clare should want to stay at home with her daughter instead of working. Clare and Lucas felt confused, miserable and unsure of what to do next. They wanted their marriage to succeed but also wanted to work in order to provide the lifestyle they had become used to. When Isabel was almost a year old they finally managed to find a local nanny who cared for Isabel two days a week. Clare returned to work full time, but needed to have several long discussions with her mother in order to help her understand why she wanted to be a working mother.

Parenthood, as Lucas and Clare discovered, not only involves the couple and their child, but also spreads ripples of care and interest through employers and relatives. It is not unusual for couples to feel that everyone they know has an opinion on how they should organise their family life! It is better to discuss childcare concerns before the baby arrives, but this does not always sort out all the issues, as Lucas and Clare illustrate. What talking *can* do is to help you rehearse how to talk about a tricky subject. This kind of discussion can also stand you in good stead when you need to deal with a particular subject later. You will have learnt how to talk about your concerns and know how your partner usually tackles certain subjects. For instance, you may discover that your partner likes to think about making a decision for a few days, whereas you make up your mind quickly. Learning each other's styles can avoid rows because you think your partner is too slow or that you are too fast. You can also try setting yourself 'mock' situations to discuss. For example, try out these ideas:

- Who will usually bath the baby?
- The baby is teething and wakes up a great deal. If you both work, how will you decide who gets up to comfort him or her?
- One of you wants another child soon after the birth of your first

child. The other wants to wait a few years. How would you decide who will get their way or how to reach a compromise?

- Your parents want to visit most weekends to see their grandchild, but you both need the weekends to be together. What will you decide to do?
- One partner wants to stay at home with the baby. How will you manage your finances if this represents a cut in your income?

Using these mock scenarios can help you to learn about your favoured approach to particular concerns; it will also help you to face real situations because you already know how you or your partner may respond.

The career couple and their growing family

Once the challenge of a first baby is managed, you may decide to have further children. As your family grows you will face different challenges to managing work and home life. Some of this depends on the age gaps between your children. For instance, children close in age may seem hard work but can mean that you deal with the same issues all at once – choosing a pre-school, for instance. Alternatively, a bigger gap may mean that you have time to manage the issues raised by one child before racing on to new ones with a second. Whatever your decision, there are 'fors' and 'againsts' in every family choice. Whenever you decide to have children, you will have to face the inevitable – they are going to grow up! Some parents feel that babyhood is easier to cope with than toddlers, while other parents feel that older children are simpler to cope with because they are easier to communicate with. One thing is sure – older children are more vocal about what they want to do and more able to have a life of their own. When both parents work, the tasks of taking children to Cubs, swimming lessons and school discos – usually in the evenings or on Saturday mornings – can all seem an added burden if you are already tired after a busy day at work. Of course, most parents are happy to do this because they want their children to be fulfilled. But the extra strain of picking up a son or daughter from a leisure club when you just want to switch off or eat an evening meal can sometimes cause tension in a partnership. You may find it helpful to draw up a schedule which divides the tasks so that each of you gets an evening off occasionally!

Case Study

Anna and Elvis had been living together for eight years when they had their third and final child. All were under six and demanded a great deal of their time and energy. In fact, although the first two, both sons, had been planned, their third child, a daughter, had been a 'mistake'. Anna had stayed at home with their sons, but had been planning to return to work when she found herself pregnant again. Elvis and Anna had mixed responses to the pregnancy, but were delighted to have a daughter. Finances were stretched as Elvis tried to support the family on the salary he earned at a local car plant. He frequently undertook extra shifts in order to bring in more cash, but this meant that he saw little of Anna, who was also tired from caring for three toddlers. Gradually their relationship began to suffer. Their sex life seemed almost non-existent and they argued more than they had ever done before. Fortunately, Anna's sister noticed that her sister and brother-in-law were struggling and offered to have the children for the weekend occasionally. Anna and Elvis spent the first weekend at home, enjoying being alone and eating take-away food! They realised that they had found life as parents to three small children tough and that they needed regular breaks to survive the onslaught of full-out parenting. When their daughter was old enough, Anna found a part-time job at the local supermarket and money became less of a problem. Their relationship got back on track and they began to really enjoy their family.

As your children grow up, you will eventually encounter the teenage years. These can be stormy times for the happiest of families, but can place a special strain on a working couple. You may want your child to be part of a team, helping out with household tasks. They, on the other hand, may have a completely different view of being part of the family! Demands to tidy a bedroom or wash up may fall on deaf ears, causing you to wonder why you are working so hard when your efforts are unappreciated. It is not unusual for couples to feel polarised by children who attempt to play one parent off against the other during the teenage years. If you are both working, this scenario can be worsened because you lack the time to talk to each other and work out a joint approach. During this period it is important to make time to see each other and get away from family concerns – even if only for a short space three or four times a week. You can then use part of this time to talk through some of the parenting issues you may be facing, allowing you to present a uniform face to your children.

Growing older – mid-life and after

Some studies seem to suggest that most people make a reassessment of their life, and the choices they have made, during mid-life. For some people this emerges as a mid-life crisis, especially if you feel that the choices you made about work or relationships are not all you hoped for. It can also be a time when you realise that you will never make the top grade at work or pursue the career you always thought you would. For others, mid-life is a real opportunity. Children may be grown up and about to leave, or have left, home. New ways of viewing work and home life can be seen as positive and welcoming. It is not unusual for people to give up their 'safe' job to follow a long-cherished dream. For instance, Vince decided to give up work as a middle manager in a technological firm to become the full-time potter he had always dreamt of becoming while he made pots in his spare time during the previous ten years. Wanting to change the way you work, or some other aspect of your life, can be hard to explain to a partner. They may not be at the same stage as you, or only see the problems ahead rather than the pleasures.

Case Study

Barry and Wendy had been married for twenty years. They had two teenage children aged nineteen and seventeen. Wendy worked as a receptionist to a local GP, while Barry was a warehouse supervisor. Their marriage was comfortable and they both felt reasonably content until Barry hit forty. Wendy felt he changed dramatically almost overnight. He began to talk about moving house and pursuing a brand-new career – teaching sailing. Barry enjoyed sailing, but had never owned his own boat. Instead, he crewed at the local club. Wendy had always thought that Barry saw this as his 'hobby'. She knew he enjoyed his weekends on the water, but he held no teaching qualifications. At first, Wendy laughed at Barry, but he seemed completely determined to carry out his idea. She became alarmed and worried. Barry was searching for houses and looking at second-hand boats in every spare moment. The children also remarked on their father's unusual behaviour. One evening, Wendy demanded that Barry 'stop being so childish and behaving as if his stupid idea could ever really happen'. They had a huge argument, during which Barry stormed out. Over the next few months, their relationship began to nosedive. Barry accused Wendy of refusing to listen to him or take him seriously. Wendy told Barry she thought he had gone mad and could see no way in which they could carry out his wishes. After many rows, Barry left Wendy and found a flat near to the sea where he hoped to gain his exams in sailing. Wendy felt devastated by events. Neither she nor Barry had coped with the mid-life crisis that had assailed them and their marriage ended in divorce, amidst severe financial difficulty.

As in Barry and Wendy's situation, the mid-life changes that many people encounter can rock a relationship that seems settled and secure. Many people survive it, while others may take a long time to come to terms with the new way of living or behaving. This is often also the point at which an affair can occur. There is no firm statistical evidence to suggest that more mid-lifers have affairs than any other age group, but many people who seek couple counselling about an affair are in this group. There is some evidence to suggest that married, professional men are more likely to have an affair than any other group, and mid-life issues may be the catalyst to an infidelity. There is more later in this book about avoiding or surviving an affair, especially those that happen through work. But broadly speaking, affairs are symptoms of problems in a relationship, not causes. They can only take root in a situation that allows for the seed of desire for another to develop. Affairs at work are usually linked to difficulties in the partnership rather than what is happening in the workplace. It is not unusual for couples to feel that it is the affair, not the relationship issue, that is the chief problem. The partner concerned may decide to move jobs, reasoning that if the job is different the problem will be resolved. Unfortunately, the desire for an affair may return in new circumstances because the heart of the difficulty has not been resolved.

Work, relationships and later life

Many couples look forward to the time of their working life that will allow them to feel less pressured and more able to spend time together. Nowadays the traditional retirement scenario is changing. Many people no longer retire in a formal sense, moving from employment to not working. They may decide to take early retirement and use their late fifties to follow a different kind of working style – perhaps as a volunteer or offering consultancy services to others in a similar field. Others do leave work, but dedicate time to turning a hobby into part-time work, such as making wedding cakes or restoring old cars. It can also be a time of reckoning, when decisions made about pensions or other financial arrangements become clear. Some couples, unfortunately, find themselves poorly off and struggle to manage on the money available to them. All these changes can have a knock-on effect on the couple relationship – sometimes bringing feelings of renewed pleasure in being together, or causing problems because the couple are unused to their new situation.

Case Study

Louise and Ken were both in their late fifties when Louise retired. Ken stayed on in his work as a railwayman, but Louise took the opportunity to retire when the company she worked for as a clerk offered her a good deal. She had always worked hard and looked forward to her time at home. She was a keen gardener and planned lots of work in her garden. But as the months went by, she began to feel bored. Ken was still working fairly long hours and she felt cut off from the life she had enjoyed at work. She hated to admit it to herself, but she missed the regular routine of office life and her friends at work. She still met them occasionally, but at home found herself wandering from room to room, uncertain of what to do with her time. She and Ken began to bicker and Louise realised that she was taking some of her feelings out on Ken. Ken told Louise that he could not take the stress and asked her to sort out her life before their relationship became embittered. He suggested that she asked the local voluntary service agency in their small town for help. Louise approached them and they found her voluntary work in a small charity that raised funds for people with cerebral palsy. Louise found that she had a talent for organisation and felt much more content. She and Ken stopped the bickering that had dogged their relationship for several months and felt they were back on track for a better relationship as they both finished paid employment.

It is possible to avoid most of the problems that couples encounter when one partner retires, or begins to wind down work, by pre-empting the difficulties that may lie ahead. Discussing possible problems or plans some years beforehand can prevent unfounded assumptions and produce contingency plans for providing sufficient funds for the years ahead. Of course, it is better to make this kind of plan at the start of a relationship because many financial issues require long-term planning, but taking a financial 'snapshot' can be extremely useful when a couple reach their fifties. You can then analyse the strengths and weaknesses in the financial and other planning you have made. It is also important to plan for the future in terms of fulfilling dreams as well as basic necessities. For instance, you may want to visit children based overseas or move to a different kind of accommodation. Whatever you decide, communication is the key to managing these concerns, as with most other relationship situations.

Chapter review

This chapter has been about understanding why couple relationships have changed so much in the last twenty to thirty years and how this has affected couples when both work. You also recognised your personal style of relating, the important influences that you may have taken on board as you developed your relationship together, and how you can manage some of the problems that may face you as you live together and follow a career. Looking at life stages pointed you towards some of the concerns that couples face at different times in their relationships, especially in relation to work.

The next chapter will expand on the early stages of the developing relationship and look at how best to create a satisfying relationship when both partners work.

2

Building your relationship when you both work

Building a successful relationship when you are both working is an important way in which you can ensure that the relationship will succeed in the future. Starting as you mean to go on removes some of the problems that making assumptions or guesses about your partner can cause in the future. This is especially important when you both work, because it is very easy to believe that you already know what your partner is thinking or feeling when you are both too busy and pushed for time to check out what your partner really thinks and feels. This chapter looks at starting out in a relationship when you are both in work (or planning to work) and how to make sure you have the relationship you really want.

Before you meet

If you are reading this book and already in a relationship, this may seem a strange place to start. But it is not as weird as you might imagine. It is worth spending time thinking about what you want from a partnership, and how your career might fit into a new relationship. It is even worth it if you are already in a partnership, because the issues raised by your thinking could influence what you expect from any partnership and might be worth sharing with a current partner. For instance, you may want your partner to know that you intend to try to climb the corporate tree and that this means taking exams and years of study. You may want to talk to your partner about the implications of this decision for the future and whether he or she is willing to support your ambitions.

In order to help you think about what you want from a partner in the context of your future, try the following exercise.

Divide a sheet of paper into three columns, as below.

Short-term Goals	Medium-term Goals	Long-term Goals

In each column list the goals that you would like to achieve over the next five years. In your list of long-term goals, you may want to add goals that carry on over a longer period of time, but five years is probably long enough to give you a realistic sense of the future. You can use one list for every area of your life or make separate lists for different areas – work, relationships, personal achievements and so on.

Case Study

Josie is twenty-four and has just moved from her first job where she was a trainee caterer. She has taken up a new post with a company that caters for conferences and has special responsibility for customer liaison. She has also been in a relationship with Pete for eight months. They do not live together but often stay the night with each other. She is not sure where the relationship is headed, but is reasonably content to live with the current situation. When Josie drew up her table it looked like this:

Short-term Goals	Medium-term Goals	Long-term Goals
To take the next set of exams in my catering course.	To gain my catering diploma.	To have my own catering company.
To move into a slightly larger flat.	To consider buying my own place.	To own my own flat or house.
To exercise more.	To join a gym or exercise class.	To feel fit most of the time.
To have a holiday somewhere hot!	To travel more widely – perhaps on a working holiday.	To work abroad for a while.
To develop my relationship with Pete.	To discover what Pete wants from our relationship.	To find a relationship that means a lot to me.
To ask for an improved salary.	To earn a better salary with more security for the future.	To feel better off than I do at present and to be able to save rather than just survive on my pay.

Josie realised that she had placed a lot of significance on developing her career, alongside improvements in money and living accommodation. She noticed that her long-term holiday plans also involved some kind of overseas work. Of less significance was her relationship to Pete and building a long-lasting partnership with him. Her long-term goal did not mention a significant relationship with Pete, but 'to find a relationship'. This made Josie feel that she should concentrate on her working life, although she did not want to split up with Pete. She felt that she was willing to see how the relationship developed rather than push for Pete to state his intentions. She also took steps to find out where she could take further classes in catering and booked in for evening classes. Some months after compiling her list, Josie managed to take the holiday she had wanted and to ask for a small rise in pay.

If you decide to undertake this kind of exercise, it can be helpful to share it with a partner – but only if you already feel that the relationship can sustain this kind of intense sharing. You may discover, as Josie did, that the relationship is less important than your career and this may come as a shock to your partner, so tread carefully in sharing the findings from your 'goal table'. Once you have drawn up your list, it is useful to underline the most important goals. You can then turn them into a list that you can pin on a board or keep on your bedside table for regular reading. Remember that you are very likely to change your goals. Life does not remain static for very long. For instance, Josie could decide to change careers. This would doubtless change the emphasis of the goals she has listed. But it is still useful to make this kind of 'goal list' because it can show you the direction in which you are currently headed, as well as helping you to see how your relationship dovetails with work, and vice versa. You may also detect imbalances that you had previously ignored. For example, you may find that you are spending long hours at work giving out to others, but have had little training to support you in your post. Lack of support and an overload of stress at work can have a serious effect on your relationship, pushing it to the bottom of the list for your attention. Noticing these issues early in a partnership, or before you meet someone special, can give you the impetus to make changes before problems become entrenched. Creating a list before meeting someone can also help you to decide how much time and effort work may take in the coming years, so that you can be honest with a partner about the kind of relationship you want. You may alter your feelings if you fall passionately in love or feel moved to change your career, but at the very least you will have a broad picture of what you see as important for the near future.

This kind of reflection can also help you to choose a partner. For example, Suzy decided that she wanted to find a partner who would be as interested in Third World aid as she was, because she worked for an overseas aid charity. She switched her leisure activity from pubs and clubs to groups who supported her kind of work and soon met Harry who was similarly interested in the aims of Suzy's charity.

Your new relationship

When you first start in a new relationship you will probably experience the excitement of new romance. Some people feel knocked off their feet by a new lover, while others are less affected. Whatever your response, it can be a very exciting time, full of hopes and dreams, but also some uncertainties. It is common for new lovers to believe that talking about their relationship is tantamount to the Kiss of Death! The urban myth about relationships seems to go along the lines of 'Real couples do not need to talk – they know each other so well they can act intuitively and know each other's minds'. It would be nice to think that this was true, but in fact couples who make successful relationships have to spend a great deal of time talking and working out potential knots in their relationship. This is especially true of new relationships that are affected by work issues. It is better to spend time talking and thinking about your relationship and work now, rather than spend time later trying to unravel a particular issue that you have not previously discussed. For instance, you may find it hard to meet your new partner because you work an irregular shift pattern. Explaining this early on is better than trying to sort out your partner's doubts about your interest in him or her because you never have the same evening free!

Here are some ideas to help you talk to your partner about the kind of relationship you want and how your plans for, or actual, work might affect your new partnership.

- **Tell your partner about yourself**
  Many new couples are so taken up with the thrill of a new relationship that they forget to say some of the ordinary things about themselves. Take some time out from telling your new love how gorgeous he or she is to talk about your past – including family and work life. You may think these things are boring or unromantic, but it will help your partner to form a picture of the real you, giving the relationship a more solid base to start from.

- **Invite your partner to talk about himself or herself**
  Ask your partner about their life, including work issues and plans. You may be surprised at what you learn! Use open statements or questions, such as 'Tell me about your plans for the future' or 'What do you think about your employer?' as opposed to closed questions that can only be answered with a yes or no, such as 'You don't like your boss, do you?'

- **Discuss your private dreams**
  Share your hopes and dreams for the future, however unlikely. They may seem impossible to you, but your partner could see a way to make them come true. For instance, you may long to work in the media but have no idea how to make this happen. Your partner may have some ideas about contacting appropriate agencies or groups. Even if the partner cannot offer practical help, they can encourage and support you while you find a way to achieve your ideas. Many people find that if just one other person says 'Yes, go for it!' it can help them to feel that their goal is attainable.

- **Talk about the importance of work in your life**
  Some people feel that work is just a means to an end – it pays the bills and enables them to enjoy other aspects of life. For others it is all-consuming and takes up large chunks of leisure time as well as work time. If you approach work from very different viewpoints it is important to discover this now rather than long after you have both made an emotional investment in your relationship.

For instance, Maggie and Joe felt very differently about work. Maggie was in the process of getting her own equestrian school under way and often worked at weekends and evenings during the summer. Joe felt that work was a necessary evil and stopped promptly at five o'clock every evening. He and Maggie ran into problems because Joe felt that Maggie should 'lighten up' and work much less. Maggie felt that Joe simply did not understand her desire to get the business on a secure footing and they often argued because Joe wanted Maggie to go out when she had arranged to see clients. Their relationship eventually ended because they could not find an amicable resolution.

- **Ask about your partner's attitude to the future**
  Once you feel that your new relationship is becoming established you will probably begin to discuss the future. Alongside discussions about whether you want to move in together or how you feel about each other, talk about what may be around the corner for you both in terms of work. For example, you should tell your partner if you know that you are very likely to be posted abroad (as in the armed forces) or need to spend time travelling a great deal. Talk about how you might handle this kind of situation. Be practical, rather than hope that it will all work out once you are together. Discuss strategies for dealing with the particular issue. For example, you could decide to find out if you can accompany your partner on assignments that involve a long time away from home (although many firms will only sanction accompaniment if you are married rather than cohabiting). As well as thinking about the short-term effect, try to consider the influence of financial considerations, working hours and style of work on your relationship over the long term. For example, if one of you works mainly from home, this will influence the style of home you choose.

Talking about these kinds of issues may seem a little forced at first. You may even feel that it does not fit with your usual way of relating. Occasionally, it can all seem 'too much too soon' – as if you are pushing a new and uncertain relationship into a more fixed partnership. But lots of new couples do spend hours talking about each other. The excitement of falling in love can be all about sharing ideas and hopes for the future – perhaps things that no one else has ever guessed you wanted. Talking about your career plans and work prospects should fit naturally into these kinds of conversations. It is true that talking about the future may need careful timing. You would probably not want to have an intimate discussion about accompanying your partner on business trips on the second date! But eventually you will get round to talking in a deeper way, when using the suggestions above could lead into discussions about your relationship and your careers.

Potential problems

Once the glow of the early partnership has passed, it is not unusual to discover that couples encounter problems. This can be the equivalent of moving from cloud nine to the real world. You may think your partner is wonderful in every way until you live together and he leaves his dirty socks on the floor or she never pays a bill on time! To some degree, this is natural. Nobody can live in the heady atmosphere of romantic love for ever. You must get to grips with the world as it is and this requires adjustments for both of you. These kinds of concerns can be mild and hardly noticeable – skirmishes over the washing up or which film to see, for instance. For others, they represent major alterations to the relationship, such as coming to terms with a partner who is often in debt.

Case Study
Molly and Keith had been going out together for about nine months when they decided to move in together. Both had been in committed relationships before, although neither had children. Keith had been married for four years when his wife died of cancer. Molly had been through a traumatic divorce after discovering that her husband had had a number of affairs. Both were wary of starting again with someone new, but had fallen in love after attending a seminar

connected to the service industry in which they both worked. They were very happy together except for something that Molly found hard to come to terms with. Keith worked for his parents' business, having done so since leaving school. Molly felt that Keith's parents were very demanding of him, often asking him to work more hours than the other staff and sometimes asking him to take a cut in his monthly pay to cover a loss elsewhere in the company. Keith appeared to accept this, telling Molly this was how it had always been. He explained that one day the company would be his and that he felt he had to earn this privilege. Molly saw it differently, feeling that Keith was often taken for granted and expected to meet his parents' demands rather than have his own needs met. Molly began to tell Keith how she felt, often angry at another evening's plans ruined because Keith had felt obliged to stay late at the office. He responded with irritation, sometimes privately comparing Molly to his first wife, whom he felt had understood his special responsibilities. To make matters worse, Keith's parents realised that Molly was opposed to their demands on him and began to suggest to Keith that the relationship was not really suitable for him. Molly felt under attack and Keith felt pressurised. The relationship soon began to drift into serious trouble, with frequent rows between Molly and Keith. Eighteen months after they began living together, Molly moved out of their shared home. Both were very sad that their relationship had failed, particularly as they had wanted a successful partnership after the sadness of their past relationships. Neither had recognised the need for negotiation of an established situation (Keith's place in his parents' company) or the effect this might have on a new relationship.

If you do encounter this kind of 'reality slump', do not make snap decisions! Once you have been through this phase you will have a stronger relationship that can withstand the ups and downs of everyday life. The adjustments you make now can help you to understand your partner and the relationship better. Here are some ideas on managing the change that this phase may bring.

- **Think practically**

  If you encounter difficulties you may be tempted to accuse your partner in a vague way of 'not caring' or 'being lazy'. Instead, be specific about your concerns. For instance, Erica felt that Owen spent too much time socialising with his work-mates rather than spending time with her. She avoided saying 'You're never here' or 'I'm fed up with being alone'. She used a specific approach saying 'I would like you to stay in on Wednesday evening so we can watch a video together'. This approach can prevent arguments from escalating and gives a partner room to reply to a request or suggestion. It also prevents your partner's hackles from rising as they are not batting back an insult or slur on their behaviour. You may *feel* angry or hurt, but you can share this more calmly once you have negotiated on the issue to hand.

- **Look at all the options**

  When couples encounter problems it is common for them to see them in black and white – leave or stay, agree or disagree, fight or apologise. But an adversarial approach to your relationship can mean that you never resolve a difficulty. If you are having problems that you are finding hard to untangle, try the following exercise.

Step 1

Find a time when you can be alone together, without interruptions, and write the issue on a piece of paper. Try to encapsulate it in a few words or a simple sentence. For example, 'We cannot decide who should take the car to work' is succinct and describes the problem, rather than a rambling essay on every row you have had over the subject of your choice. Put this paper on the floor or table.

Step 2

Next, using a shared sheet of paper, write down every possible choice you could make to resolve the issue. Add in the wacky as well as the sensible. For example, you might add 'buy a second car' even if you know you could not afford it, or 'investigate public transport' because this is a reasonable thing to do in the circumstances. Try to put aside personal preferences for a particular viewpoint. Aim to come up with at least ten options, and hopefully more. Space the options out well on your sheet of paper and then cut them out. Lay them around you on the table or floor.

Step 3
Now grade the options. You may like to have a wish list – that is, options that are attractive but not tenable at the moment. Put these to one side. Now, as individuals rather than as a couple, give each option a grade – one for 'no good' and ten for 'a great idea'. Write your grades on the options and then add them together. This will give you an automatic listing system which shows you how you feel about each option as a couple. For instance, 'one person to walk to work' may have registered as an option in your discussion about sharing the car, but only scored two or three on your personal scale. Eventually you will be left with three or four that score highly.

Step 4
You can now talk about these in turn. For example, you may find that 'create a car rota', 'each partner to travel by bus on alternate days' and 'look for work colleague who travels in my direction' come out as the highest scoring options. You may decide to take action on all of these in order to solve the problem. You could look for a colleague with whom to car-share, decide to travel by bus one week and car the next, or even discover that you could both use public transport. This kind of strategy means that you can avoid repeating the argument over who uses the car when, whilst also finding a way of solving the problem without creating winners and losers.

• *Plan ahead*
  Avoidance of a difficulty is always better than trying to tackle a problem when it has already hit you. No self-respecting moun-taineer would set off to climb Everest without being properly prepared. The same is true of relationships. The more planning and discussing you do now, the better prepared you will be to manage the problems that hit you further down the road. If you

decide to move in together, work out the nitty-gritty as well as the romantic. Deciding who will pay the rent and buy the shopping may not seem very enthralling, but making these decisions early on can avoid misunderstandings later. You could also decide to seek advice from friends or family on how they handle certain issues, but ultimately you must make arrangements that suit the two of you. These may be different from everybody else you know or similar to friends or family. Whatever the case, use the best advice for your circumstances. Do not be afraid to seek professional help for your situation. For example, if you decide to cohabit and are in any doubt about your rights over rent or shared property, see a solicitor or consult a Citizens Advice Bureau (see Further help at the back of the book) for expert help.

- **Seize new opportunities**
Sharing your life with each other can support you in making decisions about your career and lifestyle. For example, you may decide that you want to boost your career by undertaking a period of study once you have established yourself in your chosen situation. Your partner may be willing to undertake household tasks while you study, or even contribute more to the finances of the relationship in order for you to attend the course of your choice. Working as a team can open up new ideas that you might have been unable to achieve alone.

Case Study
Matt and Sheena married after living together for six months. Sheena was a management trainee, while Matt worked in administration at a local car factory. Sheena's father had recently died, leaving her a nest-egg that she decided to use to buy some property. Sheena felt unsure of how to do what, but Matt took on much of the donkey-work, taking legal advice and dealing with the practical matters of the purchase. Once the house was bought, Matt used his holiday leave to refurbish and decorate it. With a busy time at work, Sheena knew she would never have had the time to take on the house and all the work it involved. Their joint approach and

teamwork enabled them both to take an opportunity that Sheena would almost certainly have delayed for years if she had been alone.

Learning from the early days

Even if you plan your relationship carefully, you are bound to make some mistakes, as well as gaining pleasure from your successes together. Making mistakes can sometimes feel like a set-back or, in the worst situations, a signal that you should not be together. But most difficulties have the potential to be a chance to learn more about each other or even point the way to a new path for the two of you. For a couple who are both working, this anxiety can be heightened if they lack free time to discuss important issues in the way they would like. Here are some of the most common areas for difficulties to develop, with some ideas about resolving them.

Money

Many couples report money as the number one contentious issue between them. Financial problems can cause a great deal of misery, especially if you are arguing or unhappy because one partner has lost their job or you cannot find work and money is in tight supply. Alternatively, you could both be living on starting salaries as beginners in work; have got together in a second or subsequent relationship and be managing financial responsibilities to children or ex-partners; be facing an unexpected pregnancy; or simply be juggling the family budget. A Relate survey shows that people who argue about money, and earn more than £20,000 per annum, also argue more about work and housework than those who earn less. This may be because, although they are more financially secure, they are more stressed by greater responsibility at work and less able to give time at home. Money also has an important attribute in relationships – it can tell you things about your relationship you never knew. For instance, if you secretly keep a savings account that your partner does not know about, however you rationalise it to yourself, you probably do not completely trust the relationship to succeed. If you are constantly giving money to your partner (or footing the bill for meals out and shopping expeditions) with little return, you are putting far more into the relationship from an emotional point of view than your partner. In a sense, you are making an investment into a very uncertain savings account and you may find that your investment never pays off. If both of you insist on keeping the details of your financial situation secret from each other, you may be telling each other to maintain an emotional distance rather than diving straight into a romantic liaison. You may also have been hurt in the past by someone you trusted a great deal. Money can stand in your relationship as a potent metaphor for your emotional feelings towards your partner or your depth of involvement.

The most common arguments over money are usually based on how couples decide spending priorities. What you think is right to buy may well not be what your partner thinks is right! You may think the latest video recorder is a 'must have', but your partner may think it is a waste of space. Make sense of your spending priorities.

- Fix a time to create a list of absolute necessities you must have for the coming year. Choose a date to do this – January is an obvious month, but you could choose any other time, such as the new tax year or the start of a new school term. List all the things you know may need replacing, or new items you know will be needed in the coming year. For example, Tina and her partner Bruce decided to buy a small second-hand car because she would be taking their daughter to school and Bruce left early in the morning with their shared car. You will not be able to budget for disasters – such as a mortgage rise or broken washing machine – so cut some slack in the system to allow for this kind of unforeseen event. You may not always agree on what constitutes a 'necessity', so use negotiation and compromise to decide on a few key items rather than making a huge list.

- Shop together with a goal in view. You can avoid many rows of the 'Why on earth did you choose that model/colour/style/cost?'

variety by always shopping together for items on your necessity list. It may take a little longer, but you can be sure that you agree on the right choice. If you have to delegate one partner to buy alone, write down decisions about spending limits and make of item and take this with you. Stick to your agreement, even if a bargain tempts you. Alternatively, agree on spending zones in the home. For instance, you may have an eye for soft furnishings and décor so that your partner is happy for you to buy this kind of thing. If you do this, make sure that your partner has some personal buying zones as well – such as buying for the garden – to maintain a balance.

If you argue a lot over money, ask yourself what it means to you and what it may be telling you about your relationship. Look for win/win outcomes rather than one partner always ending up as the loser. If one partner has their way on a particular issue, make sure that the other partner has their choice next time to balance this.

Sex

There will be more on this topic later in the book, but you may wonder why I am suggesting that sex has the potential for problems in a new relationship. New partnerships are stereotypically seen as the point at which sex is best – spontaneous, passionate and exciting. But the truth is that sex in a new relationship may often not live up to this media cliché. You may both be tired after a long day at work, unsure about your new commitment or just learning what you both want from a sexual relationship. When you are both following a career, finding quality time alone can be at a premium, especially if you are both working extra time at evenings and weekends. But don't panic! Here are some ideas to help you enjoy sex with your partner:

- Put time aside to be with each other. If you already spend time at the pub or squash court, think about your priorities. If you want a fulfilling intimate life together, you must set time aside for it to happen. Do not worry that this is 'unromantic' or 'too planned'. If you wait for the perfect moment to make love, it can sometimes be weeks before both of you feel ready. Seize lunch breaks or early mornings if you can.

- Be affectionate towards each other as much as possible. If you are both rushing off to work, grab a few minutes to say goodbye and exchange a kiss. Greet each other at the end of the day with a hug and spend a few minutes over a cup of coffee talking about your days. These small things can be important because they oil the wheels of closeness and help sex to be more natural.

- Accept that sex is not a tap that you can just turn on. To want to make love you have to feel that the whole of your relationship is reasonably satisfying. If you spend a lot of time arguing or hardly see each other, sex will take a back seat. Men and women tend to see this issue slightly differently. Men are less influenced by the state of their general relationships and seem to be more able to separate sex from other concerns, whereas women tend to see sex as a whole package in the relationship, feeling less content to make love if the relationship has been stormy. However, both men and women would probably agree that sex is linked to the strength of the partnership and more satisfying when they feel secure.

Housework

The division of domestic chores has always been a subject of debate for men and women, and this is definitely true for couples in the New Millennium. The blurring of roles for men and women (see Chapter One) has meant that traditional ideas about what constitutes men's work and women's work have all but disappeared. While this gives men and women greater freedom to take on new roles in the world of work, it also means that negotiation about who does what in relationships can be hard to handle. Housework is the issue that lots of couples find hardest to negotiate about.

For instance, Kelly and Tim both worked shifts at the same factory. Kelly felt annoyed that Tim left his washing up in the sink for her to discover on her return from work, while Tim felt irritated that Kelly hardly ever bought milk and bread on her way home. Their problem was exacerbated by their lack of shared time. They worked shifts that meant they saw each other only briefly in the evening and mid-morning.

Manage housework issues more effectively by using the following strategies.

- Work out who is best placed to do what. For example, Kelly and Tim might have solved their problem by swapping tasks – Tim to shop and Kelly to wash up. You may have developed expectations of a partner that are unrealistic, so be more pragmatic – look at what needs doing and decide who has the most time, better attributes or the most inclination to undertake the task, rather than who *should* do it. For instance, you may feel that whoever dirties plates should wash them. But this may not be practical. Share household chores in practical ways rather than according to a complicated ethical code that you will probably disagree about! It is also important to avoid getting hung up on what a man should do or what a woman should do. Nowadays, these arbitrary divisions simply do not hold water – men should be able to iron a shirt and women should know what oil to ask for at the garage.
- Be willing to learn. If you have never cooked a meal or checked tyre pressures, ask your partner to teach you how to do these things. If your partner is unable to help you, consult your family and friends so that you can pick up the skills you may need in your new committed relationship. You can also use books, videos and other tools to help you acquire new abilities that can benefit your relationship. It is not really an excuse to say 'But I've never boiled an egg, let alone cooked a whole meal'. Start with a simple recipe book and improve your skills. You may never make chef standard, but occasionally putting a meal in front of your tired partner could make all the difference in a relationship. If you find that you are putting more into the housework than your partner, do not suffer in silence. Explain how you feel and talk about why the imbalance has occurred. It could be that extra pressure at

work has prevented your partner from doing their fair share. You could agree to tolerate this for a short while, but make sure that you receive the same kind of care when it is your turn.

- Start as you mean to go on. Do not allow particular situations to develop by default or you may become frustrated and annoyed at your partner's lack of teamwork. For instance, Shelley was delighted to clean the flat she shared with her partner Luke when they first moved in together. She thought he was useless at cleaning and saw it as rather like 'playing at house' when they first shared the flat. A few weeks later, she was feeling used and miserable. Luke started to go out, often leaving Shelley to wash up the evening meal and tidy the flat. The relationship ended when Shelley eventually felt that Luke took her for granted and was not willing to be part of an egalitarian relationship.

- When you first get together, talk about how you will divide up the daily tasks that need to be undertaken around your shared environment. Do not wait to discover what will happen once you are together, or you may find that you end up doing things you hate.

- Establish a routine. If you both know that you need to wash up every day or clean the bathroom twice a week, it is much more likely to get done because there will be a precedent for this happening. Hoping that one of you will notice that the washing is piled high in the laundry basket is a recipe for disaster. It is more likely that either one person will end up doing all the work or that both of you will assume that the other person will do it!

- Do some tasks together. You may never have thought that changing the bed or washing dishes could be fun, but you could find that this kind of activity helps to bond you as a couple. If you wash and wipe dishes together, you have a prime time to talk about what you have done that day. Changing the bed can be fun if you use the chance to roll about on it at the same time!

Socialising

It is surprising how often the subject of socialising can be a source of tension for working couples. From finding the right time to socialise to whether you like your partner's friends, you may find you disagree over a number of issues. In a new relationship it may be hard to voice your feelings on this subject, but eventually you will need to say something. For example, Michelle found that her new boyfriend Steve's friends took up too much of his time. Steve was a keen snooker player and Michelle often found him at the club when she wanted to go out with him herself. Because the relationship was new she tolerated this, but after a few months she tackled Steve. Steve was amazed that Michelle felt so strongly and agreed to spend at least two evenings at home, but Michelle felt that Steve's desire to be away from her and play snooker so often, had damaged the relationship and they had to work hard to get it back on track.

Try the following to help you dissolve these tensions:

- If you can't stand his or her friends ask yourself why you feel this way. Are you jealous of the time your partner gives them? Do they encourage him or her to behave in a way you do not like? Do you secretly think that he or she should give up friends now they have you? It is important to remember that you are unlikely to change your partner's character, so you may have to accept his or her friends as part of their life. The way we choose our friends is linked to our personal tastes and interests, so if you hate his or her mates you may be saying something about how you feel about your new partner. Are you in love with the idea of a new partner rather than the reality of their personality?
- Agree to specific evenings that are sacrosanct to your relationship. For instance, you may decide to spend weekend evenings and two weekday evenings together (or some other variation, depending on your work hours). Other time can then be made available to meet friends, attend exercise classes or a drink with work-mates without rows developing. Negotiate any changes rather than take such arrangements for granted.

Moving forward

Once your relationship is under way and you have dealt with simple decisions, you may wonder what the future of your partnership will hold. If you have decided to live together, you may consider getting married or continue cohabiting but decide to buy a place of your own. This kind of life-changing decision will be affected by your work. As you have already read, work and its influence on your relationship can be profound. It can affect how you live, where you live and the style of life you lead.

Case Study

Marie and Lewis had lived together for two years when they decided to buy a house together. Lewis was a doctor freshly out of college, while Marie was a nurse at the local hospital. They felt they knew each other well enough to take the step of committing to their own home. They had begun to investigate houses in their locality when Lewis was offered a placement at a hospital in another part of the country. Marie was pleased for him, but did not want to leave her job to accompany him. They were soon arguing over the future and unable to make a decision. Marie suggested that they should get married as this would cement their relationship, but Lewis saw this as a desperate move born out of their insecurity. He felt he could not afford to give up the placement, reasoning that it could help to provide financial security for both of them. Eventually Lewis went to the placement, leaving Marie in the house they rented. Neither was happy with the arrangement, but felt they had little choice in the circumstances. They survived the break, but it put great strain on their partnership and delayed their house purchase plans.

Analysing what you want from the future of your partnership can help you both to balance your work and your relationship successfully. Try the following exercise to help you. You could try this with a partner, or by yourself, as a guide to areas that need more discussion or action. Tick each statement that applies.

My goals for the future of this relationship are:
To develop a close relationship with my partner = 2 points
To see where it takes me = 1 point
To make a commitment to my partner = 3 points
To reassess things in a few months = 1 point

I am satisfied with the way we balance home and work issues in our partnership:
Most of the time = 2 points
Not at all = 1 point
Often OK after we discuss any problems, but then find my satisfaction declines = 2 points
All the time – we can talk easily about work and home = 3 points

We can discuss money and sex easily:
Nearly always, but do sometimes find it hard to cope with = 2 points
They are a source of embarrassment or arguments = 1 point
We try to talk about these topics, but sometimes find them hard to mention = 2 points
We can be open and honest with each other about sex and money = 3 points

We have talked about the future of our partnership:
Often and still do = 3 points
Occasionally, but not lately = 2 points
Never discussed our partnership as we believe it should find its own level = 1 point
Sometimes try to talk, but it never seems the right time = 1 point

Now add up the points. The higher your score the more likely it is that you are working on the relationship and feel reasonably confident about talking through your problems. If you have a low score it may not indicate that the relationship is in trouble, simply that you are struggling to communicate successfully. A moderate score, ten and above, indicates that you often try hard to communicate or negotiate but find it difficult to manage.

The following ideas can help you to improve your communication skills:

- Maintain eye contact. It is amazing how many people wander around the room or hide behind a newspaper while talking. You will keep the attention of your partner and be better able to explain yourself if you sit or stand on the same level as each other.
- As your partner talks, be empathetic about what they are saying. You can do this by frequently reflecting and summarising what they are saying to you. For instance, Paula listened to her husband Clive talking about his difficult relationship with a work colleague. Although he found it hard to describe exactly what he felt, Paula often asked for clarification by gently encapsulating what Clive had just explained by saying, 'So what you are saying is . . .' or 'I think you said . . .'. She remained calm and focused on Clive, which helped him to tell his story without feeling intimidated or confused.
- Do not be afraid of occasional silences. These can be helpful in communication as you both work out what to say to each other. Avoid jumping in with your own feelings and thoughts if your partner is trying to find the right way to express something.
- If your partner asks for help, try not to interrupt with lots of bright ideas. They might work well for you but be unhelpful for your partner. For example, you might be a confident person, unafraid of talking to strangers or a work superior in an open way. Your partner may be shyer and less forthcoming and feel that your approach could make things worse. Walk a few steps in your partner's shoes so that you can understand how he or she feels. Instead of leaping in with your way of coping, help them to find the way that is right for them.
- When you are faced with a difficult subject, avoid bottling up all your feelings and then talking when you both feel anxious and unable to keep calm. Instead, tackle the issue as it arises, rather than allow the concern to build up a head of steam that can destabilise your partnership. Frequent sharing of feelings can help you to keep alive a dialogue about your relationship. Gradually,

talking about your partnership will become as natural as discussing any other part of your life.

Chapter review

This chapter has been about new relationships and how they can be influenced by work and vice versa. You will have discovered how new relationships develop and looked at potential problem areas, including money, sex and socialising. Each problem was described and followed by suggestions for improving or working on a sensitive area. Learning to communicate effectively is a basis for any relationship to succeed, but especially important for new relationships. In the next chapter you can read about how to manage ongoing relationships when you both work and what steps can help you to maintain a positive partnership.

3

Moving on – maintaining a successful working relationship

Once you have established your relationship you may hope that you are now over the initial stages of becoming a couple and will begin a smooth path to a settled and secure future. But keeping your partnership on track needs you to work on the relationship every day. This is particularly true for career couples. After the excitement of finding a partner and realising that you want to make a committed relationship with them, you will meet the reality of being with someone over a long period. You will need to learn negotiation skills and tackle time management issues. Imagine that your relationship is a bank account. In order to keep the relationship solvent you need to pay into it on a regular basis so that if times are lean, you can draw on the 'savings' you have both accrued. This is important as you 'move on up' together. It is easy to become deflected from your relationship into work or leisure activities at the expense of your closeness. It is also likely that you will have differences of approach according to your gender – men often approach difficulties from one perspective while women take another.

MOT your relationship

Although there are limits to the analogy, relationships are like cars. Some people run their cars into the ground, rarely having them checked over, and then begin again with another. Others choose their car very carefully and have it regularly checked exactly according to the maker's warranty. Some people always choose the same model of car, while others experiment with different styles, often according to fashion. Relationships can be very similar. You may have chosen your partner according to your preferences or beliefs, but could have been more influenced by fashion or popularity than you realise. If you lived in another part of the world, you might have been socialised to see plump women as more attractive than thin women or to prefer a man with long rather than short hair. You may tend to look for a particular attribute in your relationship – such as sexual compatibility or a mutual love of football – or always look for the same kind of person. Whatever your approach, it is important to think about your relationship and check it frequently to see what is showing signs of wear, what may need replacing and if it is time to undertake a major overhaul.

Here is an exercise to help you give your relationship an MOT:

Firstly, take a look at the overall condition of your relationship and ask yourself the following questions. Read each numbered question or statement, then rate each one out of ten according to how much you agree with it. One rates as low or rarely achieved, and ten as good and often achieved:

Are there areas of our relationship that are showing signs of wear?
1. We are able to find time to be together that includes fun and enjoyment as well as dealing with daily routine.

2. Work sometimes spoils our plans to be together.
3. We often feel stressed or tired and this sometimes affects our relationship.
4. Plans to divide household chores have fallen apart or particular tasks often get left to chance.
5. On balance, we get on well with each other's families.
6. We still share similar goals for the future.
7. Can we still discuss tricky issues without embarrassment or tension?
8. We can listen to each other as well as tell our partner about our concerns.
9. On the whole, we still enjoy a good sexual relationship.
10. Do we see our partnership as lasting into the foreseeable future?

If you score over fifty, your relationship is probably doing well, although you still need to work on specific areas to ensure that you keep it running smoothly. If you scored between thirty and fifty, you need to look at the questions with the lowest score. Are these issues dragging down your overall score? If so, then they merit your individual attention and will benefit from being talked through with each other. If you have scored low on all counts, then your relationship is running on empty and needs attention quickly before you grind to a halt.

In Chapter Two we discussed how to talk about difficult issues in a new relationship, but you might want to approach these differently in a mid-term partnership. For instance, you may feel that you have got into a particular habit of talking to each other. You may always talk in bed together at the end of the day, or over a meal. Think about whether this habit is helpful. You may be tired if you wait until the end of the day to discuss something important or be interrupted by phone calls or TV at another time.

Dos and don'ts of talking together

- Do turn off the TV, radio or CD. Trying to talk over your favourite soap opera will spell disaster for any conversation.

- Don't stray off the subject on to some other issue. It is easy to find that you thought you were talking about who should cook the evening meal, only to discover that you have wandered into discussing your partner's work problems – again.

- Do try other venues to discuss issues. Try walking together or find a quiet café where you can talk. Changing venue can also change your mind-set and help you both to feel freer to discuss alternative approaches to issues.

- Do make sure that you have time set aside for discussion. Constant interruptions from phone calls (or children) will prevent you concentrating on the subject in hand.

- Don't think you can solve everything in one go. You may need to schedule several meeting times to talk. Take the issue to pieces, rather than tackle a huge problem in one go. Small achievable goals are better than failing to find a resolution to a large obstacle.

- Do summarise what you decide to do at the end of your talk. If it helps, write down what you decided. But beware of using this as a stick to beat your partner if you find you have not carried out your decisions. Instead, go back to talking and make a new way forward. If it did not work, it might be because you agreed to something in haste or just to please each other, without taking account of its influence on your life.

- Do reflect on the emotions that you feel when you talk. If you feel miserable, angry or determined, explain this to your partner. Avoid casting them as the baddie. Do not say 'You make me feel . . .' or 'This is all your fault'. Instead, start your sentences with 'I feel . . .' or 'I think . . .'. This will make you consider what you do actually feel and think, and prevent your partner retaliating over an implied criticism of their behaviour.

- Don't drag other people into your discussions. You may think your Dad is right about your arguments over money, but it is unfair to throw his views into the conversation. Stick to what *you* feel and believe, taking into account any influences you may have had from family and friends. It is also important to assess whether these influences are really valuable or just seem so because they have been around a while and you have become used to thinking in the same way.

- Do be creative. Talking about a difficult issue can cause you to grab at the first resolution just because you are tired and have been round the track on the issue too often. Try new ideas and approaches to solve the issue. For instance, Mel and Sanjay, both workers in a shared business, felt that they had tried every way they could to find quality time alone together. It seemed that every time they booked an evening together, something needed to be dealt with in the business. Eventually they booked an off-peak weekend at a country cottage and left their mobile phones at home. They were cut off from work but felt free for the first time in months. Their relationship was dramatically improved by the experience. If you cannot afford to go away, just tell people that you are! You may then enjoy a peaceful weekend or evening in your own home.

- Do book relationship time in your diary. I know of one couple who told people they could not make meetings on their scheduled dates because they had 'the most important meeting of my week' on that day. This usually puts off pleas to change dates or times and is simply the truth – seeing your partner regularly *is* the most important meeting of your week.

Making adjustments

When you get your car back from the garage after a service or MOT, you are likely to find that certain things have been adjusted or changed. You may discover that you have new windscreen wipers or brake shoes. The timing may have been altered. It is the same for relationships in mid-term, that is, after the initial period of getting together. You may have decided that you will arrange your daily routines in a certain way or work towards particular goals – perhaps to live in a larger home or change jobs. Now that you have been together for a while, you should be able to assess whether your good intentions are actually happening. Or you may feel that there are gaps in certain aspects of the relationship which you did not realise before.

Case Study

Jackee and Ellis met when they were both working for the same branch of Social Services. They were both social workers, drawn to each other because they shared interests in work. Both were committed to their work with disabled adults and felt a natural affinity. After going out together for six months, Ellis moved into Jackee's small flat in the centre of the town where they worked. At the start of the relationship they talked about how they would manage the financial aspect of the flat and divided up various chores – such as who would cook the evening meal. After a few months in this arrangement, they realised that they felt under some strain. The flat was small, only really large enough for one person. Jackee felt cramped and resentful that Ellis took up so much space in her wardrobe. Ellis often felt that he had no part of the flat to call his own, frequently needing to ask Jackee if she was willing to share a cupboard. Their personal possessions seemed scattered around the lounge and bedroom with the result that they frequently lost items of importance. Jackee and Ellis recognised that the problems mainly lay in the size of the flat rather than anything seriously amiss with the relationship, but the annoyance factor of their small shared area put their partnership under strain. Breaking point came when Ellis lost his car keys one morning as he was late for work. He and Jackee ended up fighting, with the result that Ellis moved in with a friend for the night. When they met the next day they realised that they had to negotiate some changes if their relationship was to succeed.

The art of successful negotiation

Negotiating is an art rather than a business between couples. It has to be learnt for the context in which you find yourself, rather than regarded as a stand-off between two people. When you hear that a union and a large corporation are 'negotiating' it is often a euphemism for blood on the carpet! Couple negotiation is very different and can have long-lasting benefits for the career couple. Follow these steps as a guide to successful negotiation.

Step 1

Before you actually begin to talk about anything you plan to negotiate, consider what you are already bringing to the negotiation. For instance, you may feel guilty that you have not met the side of the bargain you promised, angry that your partner has forgotten a promise, or sad that you have to make a change to a long-held dream. It is important to acknowledge the feelings you already have in your 'emotional luggage'. No one comes to a negotiation without pre-existing ideas about what should happen or why these things should happen. Even countries negotiating peace after conflict usually have hidden agendas and ideas about how the peace should be handled, and you will be no different. Your pre-existing feelings will colour how you describe your hopes and what you hope to achieve when the negotiation is closed.

Step 2

Try to reflect on how your partner will see the situation. You may feel angry that they have forgotten the ironing for three weeks after you had agreed that this would be one of their regular tasks, but they may be so tired because of extra hours at work that they feel justified in leaving a full ironing basket. You may still not agree on their action, but thinking about your partner's point of view can help you both to negotiate without taking up opposite sides because you have failed to look at the wider picture.

Step 3

Make sure that you both want to negotiate on the same issue. This may sound obvious, but you could have got your wires crossed, or find that the topic is hijacked by a red herring that you or your partner suddenly decides is more important. Fix a time and follow the guidelines given above on successful communication.

Step 4

Lay your cards on the table. Be honest and straightforward but avoid inflammatory language that will simply make the situation hard to handle. Do not blame or accuse. Instead, say what *you* feel. Avoid prefacing your remarks with phrases like 'I suppose you think . . .' or 'I don't know why you did this . . .' as an opener to your discussions. You could try an aid to sharing the conversation, such as agreeing that whoever is holding the house keys (or other small object such as a pebble) can speak without interruption, passing the keys to the partner for their turn when they finish. Be fair about sharing. Do not hog the talking time, leaving little time for your partner to speak. You might find it helps to make a note of what you want to say, but do not read from a pre-prepared 'speech' as this will make your partner feel that you are pressurising them and are not really genuine about what you want to share.

Step 5

Ask your partner for their response. Be willing to listen. Do not make assumptions or interrupt. Ask them to explain their feelings as well as their practical points. You may feel that an arrangement you made *is* working, but you or your partner may feel uncertain about it. How you feel about your decisions is important, because it is these feelings that affect the quality of your relationships. It may seem obvious, but couple relationships are different to business relationships. Although feelings do come into business, the 'vibe' a couple share is just as important as what gets done. If you have divided the household chores absolutely equally but both feel resentful and tired, you may see the relationship as exhausting and boring, even though to the outside world it looks like a model modern partnership.

Step 6

Talk about solutions. Even if you have come to the discussion burning with a brilliant idea to solve the concern, avoid presenting it as 'the answer'. Ask your partner what they think of your suggestion and ask positively for other ideas. Of course, you may end up with your solution because it works, but you should look at all the options open to you. If you make a suggestion ask your partner, 'How do you feel about that?' This will avoid them agreeing to something they secretly know will cause trouble in the future just because they want to please you. Take your time. Do not rush if you are trying to make an important decision – such as discussing marriage after living together, or buying a home together. If you need to, have a break at this point. Sometimes feelings and ideas change as you allow them to settle in your consciousness. The old adage about 'sleeping on it' is actually very useful. (Did you know that Einstein first saw the theory of relativity in a dream?)

Step 7

Agree a trial period. For instance, you could agree to try out a change for a month or six weeks. Make sure you fix a stop time and then move to Step 8. No negotiation should be written in stone. This is easier for simple concerns, like agreeing to shop at a different time or who should do the school run, than for something more life-changing such as buying a house. But even with this kind of decision you could go through the motions. Visit estate agencies, find out the value of your property (if you have one to sell) and look at the area you might consider living in. This kind of 'rehearsal' can have a psychological effect in that it helps you to see any potential change as more real than just thinking about it in the abstract. You will also have time to develop an escape plan if you feel you have opted for the wrong approach.

Step 8

Now repeat Step 5. Talk through your feelings and thoughts. Be respectful and understanding towards each other. You could use a table like the one below to list your mutual responses.

Change/new idea we tried/considered

Practical concerns	My feelings when we started	My feelings when we stopped the trial/rehearsal	What could happen now
In this column list all the 'nuts and bolts' of making the new idea work. For instance, Jackee and Ellis (see *Case Study* above) might list new ways of creating storage in their shared flat and the costs this might incur.	In this column, note your feelings when you first talked about the issue. Perhaps you felt doubtful that it could really happen, excited at seizing a new idea, or angry that a previous plan had failed.	In this column note your feelings after talking about, or trying out, your new way of doing things. Do you feel positive, worried, pleased, surprised or unsure, or some other feeling?	In this column make some notes about possible outcomes. You might agree to carry on with the trial, decide it was the wrong approach and renegotiate or decide to return to the original plan because it actually worked better than the change you made.

If you have followed all the steps, you should be able to see some kind of progress in your decision-making. You may feel that this is a slow way of working out couple issues, or too 'false'. In some senses, talking and negotiating in this way *is* quite slow, but that is deliberate. Rushed decision-making often results in hurt feelings and wrong decisions. This is not to suggest that taking your time always demonstrates you are negotiating successfully. You may prevaricate because you want to gain power in a particular situation by making your partner wait. Or you may move slowly because you feel unsure of how to deal with the issue. Purposeful use of the negotiating process described above will ensure that you can take steps that are helpful and measured, giving both of you time to assess your position. You may feel confident enough at this stage to take positive action about the concern you have been working through. If you have encountered difficulties in agreeing or feel that your partner is entrenched in their position, read the 'problem busting' points at the end of this passage on negotiation.

Step 9

There are several clear phases to change. They usually follow a pattern like this:

- **Pre-knowledge of the need for change**
  The problem or concern already exists but the couple is unaware of it, usually for a number of reasons.

- **The dawning of realisation that a need for change is coming**
  A particular issue begins to assert itself. The couple may notice an increase in tension – sometimes inside themselves, such as feelings of irritation when the issue surfaces, and/or between the couple, at which point they may argue or feel distant from each other.

- **A decision to tackle the needed change**
  It is at this point that the pattern of negotiation outlined above is most useful. It is important to understand that both of you may be at different points in these phases, so that problems can arise from a lack of shared perspective on a particular concern. For instance, Evelyn felt that she and her partner Roger needed to sort out how often his daughter from a previous marriage visited them. Roger felt that this was not a difficulty, until Evelyn pointed out they had not had a holiday since they moved in together because Roger had his daughter to stay every school holiday and at weekends. Evelyn and Roger negotiated the problem, agreeing to take a 'just the two of us' holiday at least once a year and to have one weekend a month to themselves. Testing out new ideas is an important task in this phase because you will not discover the pitfalls until you have experienced them. If other people are involved in the process, as with Evelyn and Roger, you may need to negotiate with them in a similar way to ensure that the action you take is a shared goal rather than an imposition on another.

- **A period of reflection**
  After the period of turbulence that change (sometimes) creates, you may need time to reflect on the changes you have made. You could regard this as a 'bedding down' time as you get used to the new way of doing things or behaving. This is likely to be a calm period in your change phase cycle, but you still need to work hard to make the change successful. Stick to your promises and agreements and continue talking about your relationship.

- **The possibility of relapse**
  All change carries with it the possibility that it will not endure forever. In some circumstances this is natural – life hardly ever stands still. You will eventually want to make adaptations and 'turn-arounds' to any decision. But you may feel that your negotiation agreement has collapsed too quickly. In this case, be honest with each other and repeat Steps 1 to 8, or review the list that you constructed at Step 8. You could enter the process at almost any point, but talk this through with your partner first.

- **The change is satisfactorily achieved**
  If you reach this point, the change is usually well integrated into your lifestyle and you may eventually forget that things were ever different. This process of change is one that you can observe in many different situations around you. Take something simple such as filling in a difficult form – a tax return, perhaps! At first you may know that the form needs doing but put it off. Then you decide to tackle it, having been nagged by your partner, a relative or your conscience to get on with it. Then you actually try to complete it, reflect on what you have done, make any necessary adaptations and send it off. You may find that there is a jump from wanting to change to actually taking action, but this will usually happen when the impetus becomes great enough – for instance, when you receive a tax demand!

It could help to try and understand where you are on the change cycle. Use the steps above to look at how you are reacting to change.

For instance, Marion and Steven decided to swap roles so that Steven stayed at home to look after their baby son while Marion returned to her job as a solicitor. They speedily took action once they had made the decision. Looking back, Steven realised they had passed through the earlier stages without realising that they had got to the action phase. They were fortunate in that they had talked about the changes that the new situation would demand, including financial and personal, for several months previously and felt well prepared for the future.

Step 10
Agree to review the situation at some time in the future. Do not be vague about this. Choose a fixed period – a few days, two weeks, a month, or longer. Whatever time period you choose, make sure you pick a length of time that suits the particular situation. For instance, if you just want to see whether your decision to divide up the household cleaning more fairly is working well, you might choose a month as a good review time. If you want to discuss a decision to move from employed work to self-employed work, you may want to give yourselves several months to gain a wider picture of how the arrangement is working.

During your review think about and discuss all the different aspects of the change you have made. Include practical elements such as finance, as well as your feelings and ideas. Be specific about what you think is working and what you want to adapt or adjust. For instance, Cathy explained to her partner that she felt they had improved the situation regarding her need to work at home in the evenings by limiting her work time to two hours an evening. This was a definite improvement on the situation that had existed before, when Cathy had tried to study erratically throughout the whole evening. Both of them saw this as positive because they were now able to spend time together without Cathy feeling anxious about unfinished essays or reading, and consequently were able to enjoy the rest of their evening. She went on to say that she needed to be able to concentrate during this time, asking her partner to avoid loud music in the evenings until she had finished her allotted two hours. He agreed that he was aware of this issue and bought CD headphones so that Cathy could study in peace.

Solving particular problems

Not all negotiation proceeds smoothly. As a couple, you may find that you disagree so vehemently about a particular subject that any attempt to negotiate is too stressful. Or you may try to implement a change only to discover that, despite promises to behave differently, nothing actually happens. These kinds of difficulties are not insurmountable, but they do require a willingness on the part of both partners to enter into the spirit of the exercise. If one or both of you comes to any negotiation with hidden agendas – such as wanting to impose your own ideas under the guise of an open mind on a particular issue – you may find that you end up in a stalemate position, with both of you stuck in a situation that does not seem amenable to change.

When you cannot find common ground

Some of these kinds of problems come not so much from a difficulty based on the action that you might take, but on the feelings you experience when you try to talk about the issue. For example, you might feel very strongly that your partner should open a shared bank account. They resist, saying that they are happy with their personal account. In this situation, think through why the shared account is important. Would it make paying bills easier, or does what you already have work? Could it be connected to a desire to feel that your partner is committed enough to the relationship to trust you with a shared account? Analysing your feelings and reasoning in this way is important because you may discover that you are protesting against the change because of some personal issue that your partner knows little about.

Next, try to see if there is one part of the change where you can find *some* common ground. Break the issue into smaller parts and talk through each part. You may discover that you can agree on most of the change by making a small adaptation to your plans. Insisting or demanding that your partner must agree to every word of your idea is not negotiation but bullying.

Agree to more frequent reviews and talk about how the plan is working in a relaxed atmosphere – over a meal or on an evening out. This will help to disarm any problems you may encounter and give you a platform to change the situation as you go along. Listen to your partner as well as talk to them about your feelings.

If you become too heated, agree some time out to cool down. Repeated arguments will only cause you to defend your position rather than enter the situation with an open mind. You may find that you tend to oppose your partner on principle rather than because they are suggesting something you disagree with. This response to a partner can be a habit that you hardly notice, especially if you have previously been in a partnership where you felt you had to 'hold your own' because you feared you would be overridden if you did not. Some possible indicators of this habit may be:

- Always looking for an alternative to even the simplest suggestions of your partner.
- Altering times and dates of social arrangements, or being late for agreed meetings and social events.
- Disagreeing publicly with your partner about past events or plans for the future. For example, Rachel often told her husband that he remembered family events in the wrong order, or told friends '. . . It wasn't like that at all. Let me tell you . . .' when he tried to tell others about a particular family occasion.
- Undermining your partner if they have made a decision. For instance, you may buy food for a dinner party that they have already catered for or insist on checking their order for a new item for the home.
- Declining sex when asked, but then asking for it yourself the next day.

This way of behaving can suggest a lack of security about the future of the relationship, or a possible hurt from a past relationship that has caused you to feel unsure of making a commitment at all. You may also have come from a family that felt children should be 'seen and not heard', so that you feel you must make an impression or be ignored. If any of these seem to apply to you, you should think about the long-term effect on your relationship if you carry on disagreeing or are unwilling to negotiate over a long period. You may both begin to wonder if the relationship can be sustained in this case, as the constant battling for answers to problems will wear you out, leaving little room for fun and pleasure.

If you always get stuck at a certain stage

You may find that you are great planners and talkers but feel unable to take action. Or you may rush to take action, but find discussing and planning boring. In either case you can spoil plans for the future by feeling stuck in a way of behaving that often fails to meet your needs. Although you can take action, it can turn out to be wrong, leaving you to sweep up the pieces of your ideas afterwards. Talking without action can leave you feeling frustrated and locked into a lifestyle that satisfies neither of you.

Counteract these problems in the following ways.

- Talk about what holds you back from taking action. Do you fear committing yourself to only one choice? Do you really want your partner to take responsibility for the action, but feel unable to say so? Could the action rebound on one or both of you, so that you fear recrimination of some kind? Understanding what stops you can be the first step to overcoming the problem.
- Before you jump into action next time, agree a pact between you that you will wait at least half a day before racing into doing something. During this time, talk about the action you want to take and explain to each other why it is important to do it quickly. You are likely to find that you run out of ways of explaining, unless you are facing a great urgency for a very special reason. Discerning whether you are facing a situation that demands an urgent response – such as paying a red telephone bill – or just

using your customary speed – such as blowing your savings on a new video – can help you to make couple decisions which will satisfy you in the future.

- Take action together. For instance, if you are concerned about the responsibility of taking action, do the task together. You may find it helpful to be physically together or to write down your decisions so that you can carry them around with you. This may sound slightly claustrophobic but it will build confidence so that eventually you will feel empowered to take action without these measures.
- If you are tempted to rush into action, spend some time talking about the things you have done quickly in the past. Choose things that worked out positively as well as those that did not go so well. Look at the positive outcomes and try to identify the behaviours that helped the decision to be a success. Did you, for instance, use the expertise of one of the partnership to make the right choice? For example, Anne relies on her partner Ned to choose computer programmes because he works in computing. Where you have made a decision that was not good, talk about the behaviours that led to that decision. For instance, did you think you had enough information, only to discover that there was a lot more you could have found out if you had delayed for a while?

If you find yourself stuck at any point in the negotiation cycle it can help to retrace your steps to discover if you can 'bump start' the situation again. You may find that if you work back to the stage *before* the problem you have encountered, you can identify the sticking point at which you either tend to prevaricate or dive for action. Both of these modes of behaviour actually avoid the difficult situation – that is, understanding and taking the right decisions about a matter of importance to both of you. 'Staying with' a difficult or uncomfortable issue might sound like psychobabble, but really only means that you are willing to face the issue before you without rushing to a solution or avoiding the reality of the topic. It sometimes means waiting for your partner to explain how they feel, testing out a different approach to an issue, or coping with uncertainties about the future. This ability to stick out tricky situations and concerns can be a real sign that your relationship is a mature one in which both of you feel able to trust your partner in a deep way. Lack of trust can cause a couple to behave in ways that are designed to avoid coping with anything that might possibly rock the security of the couple.

To use an analogy, when many couples are faced with change they try one of two things:

- they either put their foot hard down on the accelerator, speeding along to jump over the hump (problem) in the road ahead,
- or they slow down to a crawl to avoid ever reaching the hump at all.

What might actually be needed in this situation (facing and dealing with change) is to stop the car, change gear, swap drivers or take another route altogether! The process of negotiation is like reading the map before you start your journey, as well as an insurance policy for possible accidents. Once you have got used to the process of negotiation you may find it becomes easier and easier to manage, so that eventually it is second nature to you both. At this point, you may notice that your conversations naturally and effortlessly include the most important elements of negotiation and communication. Once you have reached this point, you will probably feel that you have a relationship that enables you to trust each other about most of the concerns you face, and this can be deeply satisfying.

Differences in the way men and women look at problems

It is worth noting at this point that men and women tend to have different ways of approaching problems. Of course, this is something of a generalisation, but from my observation as a couples counsellor there does seem to be a similar pattern in the way that men and women approach problem solving.

Men and problem solving

Men tend to solve difficulties by being target orientated. They see the problem as like a road, with the point they are starting from as 'A' and the resolution as 'B'. They will often set off along the road to resolution having previously decided on the most effective solution. They travel from A to B in a straight line, without trying other routes. Men tend not to involve their partner in their thinking process about an issue, but instead work through a particular course of action in their own mind and then act upon their idea. They are usually able to use this approach to be highly motivated to achieve their end, and can help to boost action in a slow problem-solving situation. There are benefits to this 'goal orientated' approach. If a problem seems intractable, taking a straight route to a solution can be helpful, if only to demonstrate that the solution is a false one. But there are some drawbacks to this approach. Men may not always recognise all the nuances of a situation and may not add in all the information they need to arrive at a resolution that makes sense to both partners.

Women and problem solving

Women are less goal orientated than men about solving problems. Women tend to see the problem as a whole landscape, with different landmarks and areas to explore. They may spend a lot of time exploring this 'problem landscape', sometimes employing a 'helicopter' approach to rise above the concern and try to see the problem from all sides. Women also tend to talk to their partner about their thought process as they head towards a solution and may also share their working through with friends and relatives. They are generally more willing than men to explore alternative solutions to difficulties, and may abandon particular approaches before they are completely clear that they have decided that the solution might be appropriate. There are some advantages to this approach. Women see problems from a holistic point of view, often understanding how people other than the couple will be affected by the proposed solution. They are usually more likely to take into account the feelings of all those concerned and to involve these people in solving the difficulty. Some of the disadvantages to this approach are that action can be hard to get off the ground because the woman may be trying to pull too much into the scenario. There may be confusion about whether the problem has been sorted out to everyone's agreement.

Although men and women may differ in their approach to problems, this can prove a hidden strength which couples can utilise in their negotiation strategies. It has been common for men and women to feel that their way of tackling problems is the 'right' way, often criticising their partner's approach. But using these different ways of solving difficulties can mean that men and women can gain from using the best of both approaches to solve couple problems. This does not mean that a man or woman's way of dealing with a problem is better than the other. It just means that, although the approaches are different, they can be used in a constructive fashion rather than a destructive manner, if the couple is willing to utilise the different strengths in order to help them understand and solve problems.

Case Study

Zoe and Jack had been married for ten years. Both had jobs at the local car firm. Zoe worked in administration and Jack was a foreman on the shop floor. Zoe had been married before and Viv, her thirteen-year-old daughter by her previous husband, lived with them. One August day, Zoe was contacted at work by the police and asked to come to the police station to collect her daughter. Viv had been caught shoplifting in the town centre with a group of other teenagers. Zoe was shocked and extremely upset. Viv was angry and in tears when Zoe picked her up and very embarrassed at having been discovered to have been shoplifting. After some discussion between the shop and the police, the shop agreed to drop charges as it was a first offence. The police gave Viv a warning and Zoe brought her home. The next few days were tense and stressful. Zoe had lost touch with Viv's real father, who had left when she was a baby. Jack regarded himself as Viv's father in every way that he felt counted and so was also upset and surprised at Viv's behaviour. Neither felt able to take long periods off work, but did want to monitor Viv during her school holiday. Viv hardly spoke and only explained herself by saying that 'all her friends did the same thing'. Zoe and Jack spent hours in the week that followed trying to decide how to react. Jack felt that Viv should be grounded for the rest of the holiday and then accompanied by them on any future shopping trip. Zoe wanted to understand why Viv had been shoplifting and was unsure that she would respond well to Jack's idea of keeping her under close watch.

At first, Jack wanted to tell Viv how he felt straight away. He felt that Viv needed to know that she could not repeat her behaviour. Zoe asked him to wait before he said anything about his decision. Zoe talked to Jack about the circumstances of the situation, including her thoughts about Viv's choice of friends and the school difficulties that Viv had experienced the previous term. Jack acknowledged the truth of Zoe's remarks but also felt that, no matter what had happened, Viv needed to understand that what she had done was wrong. He saw the problem as Viv behaving irresponsibly and that this needed punishment, no matter what the provocation. Zoe saw the problem as linked to lots of other concerns that affected how they should deal with Viv. After much negotiation Zoe partly agreed with Jack about Viv being grounded and gradually winning the right to go out alone. Jack supported Zoe in finding a youth counsellor that Viv agreed to see.

Jack and Zoe found they could use the different approaches of men and women to problems to support and help each other as they decided what to do to cope with Viv's behaviour. Viv gained from the shared response as she received a balanced attitude that was fair and met her needs for the difficulty to be faced and managed.

Solving problems with your partner if you are a man

Although you may be tempted to rush towards a solution, or to take action alone to resolve a problem, talk things through with your partner first. It is possible that you present your solution without talking to your partner about the different phases of your thinking. This can be disconcerting, as your partner may not have realised that you went through a process at all, seeing your final announcement as a bolt from the blue which she may immediately jump to counteract. All may not be as it seems at first sight, and you could benefit from hearing about how your partner sees things. This is not to suggest that you cannot use your action-based ideas later, but you may need to gain a wider picture first. Explain why you see things as you do and listen to your partner.

Case Study

Clara was trying to decide whether to give up her job as a supervisor in a retail unit and follow her budding career as a photographer. Photography had always been a leisure pursuit for Clara, but her reputation had built up until she was often at weddings and parties most weekends and taking portraits in the evenings, specialising in children. She was finding it very difficult to leave her safe job for a freelance lifestyle. Her partner, Tim, urged her to take the plunge, offering several ideas about how she could safeguard some of her financial concerns. With his positive support, Clara was able to become a photographer, something she knew she would never have done without Tim's push towards action.

Tim was able to urge Clara to action, but took into account her need to feel secure in her decision. It was Clara's decision to leave her full-time employment, but Tim was able to help with the mechanics of the change. Men can often give this action-based help to women, but it must be given without some of the traditional overtones of 'men know best'. As a man, support for your partner must be given out of respect for their abilities and strengths rather than in a bullying or hectoring fashion.

Solving problems with your partner if you are a woman

You may find that you spend a lot of time talking to friends and relations about important issues in your life but, paradoxically, less time talking to your partner about your concerns. This could be because you assume he ought to understand your way of thinking without you needing to explain in detail. But the truth is that you need to allow your partner to share in your personal approach to a problem or an idea – perhaps more so as you range across various ways of dealing with the concern. Ask him for his opinion and ideas. This can be helpful if he is more action-based in his approach than you are, because it may enable you to see a clearer way forward if you have become swamped by the numerous influences on your decision-making. You can also help him to consider all the influences on a particular issue by outlining them for him.

Case Study

David and Ellie had been together for two years when David changed jobs. At first, they were both delighted. David's new job was a step up in car sales to a management position. Things went well for about four months until he developed problems with his boss. He was extremely critical of David, often asking him to rewrite reports and ridiculing his ideas at meetings. After a particularly bad day, David told Ellie he intended to write his boss a strongly-worded letter outlining his feelings about his treatment. David was not so much angry as exhausted by the battle to make his job successful. Ellie spent the evening with David looking at all the issues surrounding the situation, suggesting that David hold back from action until he had viewed the problem from all possible angles. David and Ellie talked long into the night. By the next morning, David had decided to wait for a while to see what the situation was like in a month's time. With Ellie's support he also contacted his personnel manager and talked through the situation with her. She was able to work with David on the problem, suggesting that David consider a transfer to a nearby garage in the same chain if things did not improve. Ellie helped David to use more assertive responses to his boss, quelling the irritation that often arose when his boss started criticising him. Eventually, David did not move workplace but felt better equipped to manage the issue which soon improved once his boss realised that David was quietly determined to manage in his own style.

* * *

David was enabled to take action that utilised Ellie's support, with the result that the action he did take was effective and useful. Ellie was also involved in the decision that David needed to take in order to achieve a less stressful working environment. They gained not only a practical outcome, but also an outcome that helped them to feel like a team rather than individuals pulling in opposite directions.

Of course, this approach to thinking about how men and women cope with problems is a generalisation. You may feel that things are very different in your relationship. Perhaps you are a woman who often takes swift action or a man who talks to others about your feelings. But you can still use the understanding gained from the above examples to deal with relationships which are characterised by different styles of problem solving by each partner. The most important thing to remember is that many couples use the differences between them as the reason for not agreeing or working together to solve a problem. Focusing on the different approaches as strengths rather than weaknesses can encourage you to find a way forward.

Common mid-term couple issues

Career couples in mid-term – those who have been together long enough to develop a commitment to one another – are likely to meet some specific concerns. The following sections outline some of the particular issues you may meet.

Taking the relationship for granted

At the start of the relationship, you may have made special efforts to be dressed up and on your best (or most flirtatious!) behaviour. As you get to know one another, some of this desire to present your best side declines. You may feel confident enough to allow your partner to see you unshaven or without your make-up. This is a natural progression, since building trust in a relationship means getting to know your partner 'warts and all' rather than as someone who seems stuck on a pinnacle – lovely to look at but untouched by real life. However, you may take some liberties with your partner that undermine the sense of closeness that has developed. Career couples often encounter this as the 'you love work more than me' syndrome. At the start of the relationship you may have sprinted from the office to get ready for an evening out. Now you pick up the phone to deliver the often-spoken lines 'I've got to work late tonight' and mean that you *are* working, not meeting your lover! You may also take work home regularly or agree to after-work drinks once too often. In order to counteract this syndrome you should trade extra work times or socialising with work colleagues for an evening together or whatever event you want to attend together. For example, Louisa worked in the media and was often called on to provide support to journalists covering late-night news stories. She agreed with Greg that she would give him the same amount of time as she gave to her work. Sometimes they spent the time watching TV together, making love or going to the local pub, but it was kept as 'their' time and Louisa would put off other things to ensure that they spent the time together.

Professional jealousy

This is an issue that is hardly ever discussed in an open way by couples, or by other people for that matter, but it often affects mid-term couples where both partners work. Usually the difficulty arises if one partner is promoted, receives a better salary or simply changes their work. Both partners may start out in careers where they perceive their work situations to be well balanced. This may not mean that each partner earns exactly the same amount, or has the same kind of work, but that they accept the situation. For example, you may earn more than your partner but you both feel this is acceptable and that it is fair that your partner contributes more financially to the relationship. If you start to earn as much as, or more than, your partner, he or she may feel jealous that their 'superior' position has been usurped in exactly the same way that children can fight to be 'top dog' in a family. All of this may go on at a subconscious level and it can be shocking to discover that you feel jealous of someone you love, but these are normal feelings. Feelings of jealousy that your partner is doing better than you or has a better deal in life can be hard to overcome, especially if at least some of your self-esteem is based on a successful career or earning a reasonable salary. In a sense, this is the theme of the film *The Full Monty*. In the film, a group of unemployed men seek to prove that they are still worthwhile as partners and men, even though they cannot find a job after the closure of the steel mills in the North. For this group of men, the fact that their wives and girlfriends *do* have jobs rubs salt into their wounds. Although these feelings are natural, they can be disconcerting. Sometimes arguments about who does what in the home are partly based on this hidden jealousy. Often jealous feelings are prompted by unrealised ideas about the role expectations of men and women. Despite living at the beginning of the New Millennium, many couples unconsciously fall into old ideas about men being the chief earner and women earning less. When women earn more, or take on a prestigious job, men may feel that their self-esteem is knocked. When men do better than women, women may feel that they have not had the chance to express their similar ability. This kind of 'underground' rivalry can be painful, but it can be disarmed by raising the issue to the surface. If you encounter changes of this kind, make sure that you actually talk about the feelings that go along with the events. Alongside the congratulations on a promotion or salary rise for you or your partner, ask yourself how the change has affected the relationship.

Do not allow these kinds of feelings to stew, because you may then feel unable to discuss them openly. If you wish it were you rather than your partner who had done well, be honest but not cynical. Acknowledge that you would also like to do as well, but then look at the benefits that the change can bring the relationship – perhaps more cash available for leisure or a chance for your partner to delegate some work so they can be home more often. If you feel chronic jealousy, always wanting to be one up on your partner, you need to address your sense of self-esteem and how you gain your self-worth. Feeling good about yourself because others are lower than you is not a secure base on which to place your relationship. This is rather like pushing yourself up on the shoulders of another person and deciding that this means you are taller than they are. Use means other than your work to improve how you feel about yourself, such as pursuing an interest or voluntary work that helps you feel you are contributing something worthwhile to the world. If you know this is likely to be a difficulty for you, avoid choosing a partner in the same career as you, or make sure that you feel able to talk about work in a non-competitive way before you form a deeper commitment.

The influence of other people on your relationship

When you first set out together you are likely to be so focused on each other that other people, including friends and family, take a back seat for a while. But as your relationship develops, you will probably reconnect with those who seemed out of the picture for a while. This can also be true of work colleagues and associates, who may persuade you to return to the socialisation patterns that you followed before you met up. Watch out for a return to familiar ways of doing things that shut your partner out. Late nights drinking with friends, or long lunches which then require long hours at the office afterwards, can cause your partner to feel that other people are more important or that your sense of commitment is waning. Think about what your relationship needs now that you are together and give yourself some rules about what you want to happen now. For instance, you may agree to spend an evening a week with friends or to cut out drinks after work.

Time management issues

When you are both busy following your chosen career or working long hours, you may find that your relationship comes second in terms of time. As you read earlier, booking time to see each other is an excellent way of making diary space to create a relationship that is relaxed rather than tense. You may also need to consider how you manage the ordinary concerns of daily life such as gardening, cleaning and the routines you carry out every day. Avoid allowing these to build up so that your free time – time that you could give to having fun in your relationship – is given over to these instead. Boring as it may seem, organising in order to manage these chores will help you to have a partnership which is happier and avoids constant rows about who should have done what and when.

Chapter review

This chapter has discussed how mid-term career couples manage their relationships. The most important issue for couples who are deepening their commitment is to ensure that their relationship receives the same amount of attention that it had when the couple first got together. Learning how to assess and understand the changes that may occur after a period of time is important, so the chapter offered ideas on how couples can 'MOT' their relationship as well as negotiate about their partnership. Suggestions about the particular difficulties that mid-term couples might face, such as taking the relationship for granted, professional jealousy and time management issues, were explored, as well as the different ways in which men and women tend to manage problems.

4

Work, children and love – getting the balance right

This chapter is about one of the most difficult balancing acts that career couples undertake – how to maintain a relationship whilst juggling work and family life. For some couples the stresses and strains are huge as they try to ensure that the different elements of their lives receive the attention they need. For others, creating a balance is less problematic and can be managed with only a few small alterations to everyday life. Whatever your experience, moving from being partners to being parents is a significant life event. Adding work and your career to this change usually takes commitment, hard work and excellent communication skills.

Previous chapters have dealt with some of the basics of good negotiation and communication. Understanding these techniques will stand you in good stead for the future, especially as you approach becoming a family. But there are important concerns for career couples who want to start a family, or who are already dealing with children as well as their relationship. These are usually concerned with making choices that enable the balance in your relationship to remain steady.

Choosing children

As a couple you will need to make a choice about whether to have children or not. In some senses this is a very modern choice – properly effective contraception for most people has really only existed for about forty years. Generations of couples before you had to hope that their children would arrive at a time when they could afford it. New Millennium couples have a choice that their grandparents would have envied. This may be why the mother's age for the birth of her first child has got steadily older during recent years. Since 1992, women in their early thirties have been more likely to give birth than those in their early twenties, although the fertility rate is still highest for 25 to 29 year olds. Women are likely to postpone childbirth until they have established themselves in careers or work, rather than depending on a man to provide for them financially. So it seems that couples are making an affirmative choice about having children when they are in a financial position to do so. (Unfortunately, this does not seem to be the situation in communities in which there is poverty and unemployment, where there are increased rates of teenage pregnancies.) For some couples this may mean deciding not to have children at all. This can be difficult to explain to friends and relatives, who may make assumptions about the inevitability of you having a child. Other couples may decide that they would like children when a certain set of criteria have been met – owning a house or attaining promotion, for instance. Whatever you decide, the process by which you make this decision can be important. Without a clear understanding of how you decide about having children, you may feel that you have not explored all the options open to you. As a consequence, you may find yourself feeling resentful or disorganised as you become a parent.

Deciding about becoming parents

Talking about your feelings about becoming a parent is crucial before you get to the question of when you want to have a child. *Whether* you ever want to have children is obviously important to address before you think about *when* you want a baby. The future of your relationship may be coloured by your decision to be or not to be parents. This is especially important if you differ in your expectations of becoming parents.

Case Study

Dawn and Barry had been living together for four years when Dawn told Barry she felt ready to have a child. Barry was appalled. He had recently changed jobs and was establishing himself as departmental head of maths in a local school. He had high hopes of a headship eventually, but saw becoming a father as an interruption to these plans. He had seen himself as a father eventually, but not for several years to come. Dawn was understandably extremely upset, and they endured several days of cold silence. She had assumed that Barry would want a child as much as she did and at around the same point in the relationship. She was less secure in her job and felt that if she chose to leave it would not be a major issue and that she could find a new post as a librarian later. The issue gradually became a very sore point and the subject of numerous arguments. Dawn explained that, at 35, she felt she could not afford to wait to become pregnant. Barry angrily told Dawn that she had made unfair assumptions about their future. Neither felt able to break the impasse. The partnership deteriorated into polite exchanges rather than the intimate closeness they had previously shared. Dawn met Paul, with whom she began an affair, eventually leaving Barry a year after their differences began. She and Paul moved in together and married when Dawn found she was pregnant two years later.

Dawn and Barry suffered because they failed to undertake the most basic communication about their relationship and parenting. You may think you know how your partner feels, or believe they will agree with you because you have agreed about other matters, but it is vital to check out responses and expectations relating to parenting long *before* you decide it is the right time to become a parent. Here are some strategies that you can use to ensure you understand each other on this subject.

- Talk about whether you want to have children at all. Use all the information known to you about the future and your plans. You might find it useful to draw up a list of pros and cons. Be honest about any misgivings and explain why you feel as you do. Your list might look something like this.

Fors	Againsts
A child would complete our relationship and demonstrate our love for each other.	We are tight for cash. We can't afford a baby.
I have always enjoyed having children around.	I often have to work from home. A crying baby would be hard to handle.
If we had a child now we would still be young enough to continue our careers in a few years' time.	As the mother, I might have to give up work for an extended period of time.
I have always seen myself as a mother/father.	I came from a family that did not treat children very well. I am worried about being a parent myself.
I enjoy playing with children.	I hate the idea of changing nappies.
I could do some freelance work while the baby is small.	Being a parent means giving up holidays and evenings out. I do not want to do this.

Once you have drawn up your lists, discuss the items you have outlined. You may find that you can wipe out some immediately if you both suggest ways of coping with the issues concerned. For instance, you may agree that if you do a role swap, with the chief earner working and the less well paid staying with the child, you can overcome the problem of who cares for the baby. Alternatively, you may feel that if you both have enough 'againsts' you should definitely not have children. A third option might be to review your decision at a fixed time in the future. This allows for the possibility of change and builds safeguards into the decision-making process. However, it is dangerous for one partner to hope that the other will change their mind and so hang on to the review as a indication that their partner will think differently at a later date. If you both have very different agendas – one wanting a child and the other not – you may discover that the relationship is hard to sustain. It is not always the case that the relationship will fail, but it can be hard to overcome such a fundamental difference in expectation. It is better to know this at the beginning of the relationship rather than wait to discover it much later when you are both deeply committed to the partnership.

- If you make a mutual decision not to have children, think about what you want from the future of the relationship. Couples can sometimes see having children as a creative act, and although couples without children are as creative as couples with children, it can sometimes be hard to find this creative factor in the relationship. Allow space for the development of creativity – whether it is arts based or connected to work. When talking to others about your childlessness, explain that it was a mutual decision and that it has allowed your partnership to develop in the way you wanted. Other people may criticise because they feel threatened by your alternative decision. Your choice to be a parent is your choice alone. Nobody else has the right to suggest you should do something differently if that is not your choice.

Deciding when to have a child

If you have discovered through discussion that you do want a child, the next issue will be deciding when this should happen. It is at this stage that many couples find themselves caught in a set of difficult issues.

Here are some of the contributory factors that influence couples making the decision to have a baby.

- **The age of the couple**
  This is clearly important from a health point of view, but can also indicate that you have a limited time period in which to make up your mind. This can be particularly true for couples in second or subsequent marriages, or where the couple is older when they get together. Talk about how you will feel if you are older parents or wish to have other children after the birth of the first child.

- **The stage of career reached by one or both members of the couple**
  If you have taken several years to climb the corporate ladder or recently obtained a job with good prospects you may be reluctant to take the chance that things will still be the same when you return from maternity/paternity leave. You may find it useful to talk in confidence to your personnel officer about becoming a parent and check out the legal position regarding your job. For instance, the amount of time you have worked for an employer can affect the amount of maternity leave you can have. (Contact the *Maternity Alliance* on 0171 588 8582 for a variety of information about the rights of parents who work.) It may be comforting to remember that if a company has invested in you as an employer they have a good reason to support you through the early days of parenting. Losing you would mean retraining another person from scratch.

- **The financial situation of the couple**
  Some couples seem to be able to manage large families on a shoestring and remain perfectly happy. Others struggle on their income and feel that the added financial stress spoils their family life when the child is born. You need to think about the financial implications of having a baby. Once the child is born, the impact on your wallet will not shrink and is likely to grow! Take a look at your bank accounts and savings. Assess the way in which a possible reduction in salary will affect you. If you both decide to go on working, add the cost of childcare in to your sums. Once you have done this, think through any long-term costs that are not immediately apparent but could be if you delay having a family. For

instance, you may have elderly parents who will need your care in ten years' time. Could this have an impact on your financial situation? Try to talk about the subject in actual terms rather than as abstract ideas. Use scenarios to help you both feel in touch with the situation. For instance, you could talk about whether having a child would mean you stop having foreign holidays or if you would need to save more than you do currently. You might also try balancing the financial cost against the importance to you of having your son or daughter. You could feel, for example, that you will save less or need to cut down on work hours, but that this will be worth it for you to become parents. Or you may feel that you have suffered a great deal of financial hardship over recent years and you are not ready to face this again.

- *The sense of commitment of the couple*
  You may believe that you are totally committed to one another and that this is an erroneous question to ask yourself. But it is surprising how many couples go into parenthood feeling ambivalent about their relationship. Even if you have been through a formal marriage ceremony, you may still wonder if the relationship can sustain the impact of a child. Most divorces occur between five and nine years after the marriage – the point at which the majority of couples start a family. The tension that even stable relationships experience when a child is born can be extremely surprising. Talking about commitment is not easy. Who wants to admit that their partnership could topple? But you can talk about how you think you will feel if a child comes along. It can be useful to look at other situations where there is a rival for your attention or affection. How do you feel when something or someone takes your partner's interest? Can you be jealous or feel pushed out? A child will amplify this experience so you need to understand why you feel this way and take steps to remedy your feelings. This kind of problem is often linked to a lack of self-esteem, so consider if you need to work on improving your sense of self-worth. Some couples also employ the 'superglue baby' syndrome – that is, they decide that the best thing to shore up their failing partnership is

to have a baby, reasoning that this will bring them closer together. Unfortunately, the stresses and strains of having a child are much more likely to cause you to part rather than stay together. It is also unfair to expect a child to carry this degree of responsibility for an adult relationship.

When thinking about having a child, avoid having a baby to please other people or because you have reached the age when all your friends are having a child. Pressure from relatives and friends to take the step to parenthood can feel overwhelming, especially if you have already had some vague thoughts about becoming parents. You may also hear the ticking of your own biological clock if your friends of a similar age begin to have children, and this can make you feel as if you should be behaving in the same way. Talk about any potential pressures and decide if they are relevant to your thinking. Compare similarities and differences between you and your friends. For instance, you may be of a similar age, but you might have forged ahead into management while they have been happy to stay in a different situation. You may be less or more well off or with a partner who already has children by a previous relationship. All of these are of equal importance when thinking about having a child, so do not be swayed by a friend's opinion that it is time you had a family!

Pressure from relatives can be harder to counteract. You may want to please your parents by having a grandchild, but it is you who will ultimately have to bring a child up. Rather than end up with a stand off with your parents, explain carefully why you can or cannot have a baby at the moment. Be straightforward and firm, saying that you will take the decision when the time is right for you. If you decide to put off having a child for a while, you may have to endure arguments of the 'Well, we only had a little cash when we had you, but we managed' variety. Just stick to your guns in a polite way and eventually the remarks will probably diminish. This is perhaps the most important decision of your life – do not be afraid to think about yourselves and what is right for you in your personal context.

Career couples during pregnancy

Assuming you have decided to have a child, and all goes well with conception, this can be both an exciting and difficult time to manage. You will be pleased to have a baby on the way, but probably also managing dual careers. Not all pregnancies are straightforward, and even those that are require the woman to take time off from work to attend regular check-ups with the medics caring for her and the baby. Women are entitled to paid time off for antenatal care. This covers not only the actual appointment, but also the travelling time to and from the appointment. This is true no matter how short a time you have been employed or how few hours you undertake. Your employer may wish to see written evidence of your pregnancy. If you are denied these basic rights, you can institute a claim to an industrial tribunal within three months. Your employer should conform to new legislation by ensuring that your workplace is safe for you to work in. If this is not possible, you should be offered reasonable alternative employment at the same place of work. It is important that you know your rights under the law both during your pregnancy and at the time of the birth of the child. Ask your GP for a copy of the NHS Patients' Charter, which outlines your rights to specialised care during pregnancy and birth. You should also ask your employer or personnel officer for details of your rights to maternity and paternity leave, pay and salary during your pregnancy, plus information about returning to work after the birth. If you feel secure about your working conditions while you are pregnant, you will probably both feel less worried about the future. Lack of support at work can cause you to take out your anxieties on a partner, so it is worth doing your homework to make sure that you start out well on your journey to parenthood.

The attitude of other workers

You may find that your pregnancy affects other people that you work with. Most colleagues will feel pleased that you are expecting a child and offer support during your working day. Do not be afraid to grasp offers of help with tasks that may prove difficult while you are pregnant, such as lifting heavy objects. (If this kind of task is routine in your job, the law says you should be able to relocate within the same firm or take a suspension on full pay if no alternative is available.) Some colleagues can prove unsympathetic to pregnant women, and you may find yourself trying to prove that you can do exactly the same work as anyone else. You will probably not do yourself or the baby any good if you adopt this attitude. Try to see the pregnancy as an ideal opportunity to reassess the way you work. If you work long hours, you should go home at a reasonable time and relax. Eat a proper lunch, including fruit and carbohydrates to get you through the day (a bar of chocolate does not count!), and have at least a half-hour break, preferably away from your desk. A stroll in the local park at lunchtime might also help any back pain caused by the growing baby. Make sure you have a well-adjusted desk and chair for your changing shape and stay away from smokers. (Ask for a smoking ban if one does not already exist under health and safety regulations in your office.) Improving your personal working practices might provide the best example to push colleagues into working in a more family-friendly way. If you run into problems with a specific colleague, try to use some of the skills outlined earlier in the book to negotiate on particular issues. If you still cannot solve work concerns after using this technique, talk to your line manager or personnel department. It really is important to remain calm and unflustered; stress will not only affect the baby, but may also spill over into your relationship.

The role of the father during pregnancy

Just as the pregnant woman needs to find out about legal, medical and employment rights during pregnancy, the father-to-be also needs to explore his rights at work. Some companies will allow fathers to accompany their partners to antenatal appointments or classes as well as giving paternity leave once the baby is born. Others operate different schemes that are less flexible. Talk to your employer or personnel officer early in the pregnancy, perhaps after the first three months, to ensure that you are clear about your rights and your employer's attitude to your partner's pregnancy. You should also support your partner from an emotional and practical point of view. As a career woman she may be tempted to believe that she needs to work in exactly the same way as before she became pregnant. Of course, each woman's attitude to her pregnancy will be different. Some will sail through, hardly noticing any difference to their physical or emotional selves. Others feel rough from the start and need more care to get them through the nine months. In this matter, you are placed in a unique situation. You know your partner intimately and will be well placed to notice the small changes that others may miss. Not only is it important to encourage her to relax, eat properly and take moderate exercise during the pregnancy, but you also need to help her to see the pregnancy as preparation time for the early months of parenthood. If you both arrive at the labour ward exhausted and stressed out because work has taken a toll on you, the birth of your child may seem like another problem rather than the joy it should be. In order to be ready to be a father, you also (like your partner) may need to take a long cool look at your working practices. If you work all the hours available, bring work home or work tough shift patterns, now is the time to overhaul these practices. With the birth of your baby, you will be transformed into a man who has a set of responsibilities other than work. Your partner and child will require lashings of attention, play and fun over the coming years. This kind of quality attention is not achieved if you are constantly at the office or in the factory. No one ever says at the end of his or her life 'I wish I had spent more time at the office'!

Preparing for the birth

As the time of the birth comes closer, you should both talk about the arrangements for the birth. First, make sure you are able to contact each other easily so that the father can reach the birthplace in time. Mobile phones and pagers are a great help here. Otherwise, make sure you both know where you are during the day as the due date draws closer. As the father, you should negotiate with your employer about attending the birth. It would be a very hard-hearted boss who said you should take the time away as unpaid leave, but it is wise to check what the company expects. Whether the father stays with his partner during the birth or waits outside the birth room is a very personal decision. As with other issues about having a child, avoid caving into 'shoulds' and 'oughts' from other people. Whatever is right for you is the right thing to do. But do spend some time explaining to each other why you feel the way you do, in case your partner makes assumptions about why you will or won't do something. For instance, Shan told his partner that he would not attend the birth because he felt he could not cope with the blood. He had a phobia about blood and often fainted at the sight of it. She was disappointed, but understood his reasons for his choice. Shan came in to see the baby as soon as it was born, and this worked for them. Whatever you decide, work should not come first. It is not unknown for fathers to continue to work up to the last moment and even try to conduct business conversations on mobile phones at the bedside! This is obviously an extremely bad idea. Not only will the father be stressed and inattentive, but his partner may also wonder who comes first in his affections – her or work!

Your relationship

If you have both worked right up to the birth, taking only the bare legal entitlement to maternity leave, you may have mixed feelings about the time off for the birth. This can be especially true if you have responsibilities at work that are hard to relinquish, or if you are self-employed. But the arrival of a baby in your life is a revolution. The event is sometimes likened to the neutron bomb – leaves buildings standing but in every other way destroys life as we know it! If you can approach the birth feeling reasonably relaxed, rather than fraught with anxiety about work, it will pay dividends for both you and your partner. In some senses, this time is a watershed in your relationship when you have time to talk and learn about the new roles that you are about to undertake. Use this time to discuss how you feel about becoming parents, how you will maintain your relationship as the child grows and what expectations you have of your working life in the future. It might also help to increase your physical affection towards one another. I am not talking about sex as such (although this might also improve your sense of bonding, if your GP agrees it is safe to make love) but more about displaying warmth towards one another. Here are some ideas to build affection as you await the birth of your child:

- If you are watching TV or a video together, sit close to each other and hold hands or cuddle. If this proves difficult because of the woman's 'bump', adjust your position so that you can be close in comfort.
- Offer a massage to each other. A neck and shoulders massage can be very relaxing as well as affectionate. The woman may appreciate a lower back massage or more gentle stroking on her stomach. Massage oils can be very pleasant, but read the instructions carefully as not all of them are suitable for pregnant women. If in doubt, ask the shop where you buy them, the pharmacist or your GP.
- Tell your partner how much they mean to you and how proud you are to have them as the father or mother of your child. Dream a little about your hopes for the future as a family. It does not matter if your dreams are realistic or not – the object is to talk about your ideals for the future.
- Give a small gift or card to your partner. Flowers or a simple love note can really lift a day. Pregnant women often feel unattractive at the end of their pregnancy, so a small token of affection can be a real boost.
- Make sure you spend time together that is uninterrupted by work concerns. This is particularly important if you work from home.

Financial considerations

With the birth of your child imminent, you should discuss your personal finance and how this will be arranged in the future. If you are cohabiting rather than married it is important to sort out any unclear areas of your financial arrangements. Under the law, co-habitees do have fewer legal rights than married couples, especially in regard to property and parenting rights. You may find it useful to visit your solicitor to ensure that you are clear about your entitlements and to tidy up any loose ends regarding your finances etc. But for any couple, married or not, it is useful to 'spring clean' your finances and make sure that you are satisfied with your current arrangements. Tidy up how you pay bills and who pays for what. For instance, you might find it beneficial to arrange direct debit for regular bills so that trying to remember to pay the electricity bill can be one less thing to worry about as you grapple with washing babygros and visiting the baby clinic! If you do want to return to work after the birth of the baby, ensure that you have alerted your employers to your intentions and taken advantage of your benefits. If you intend to return at the end of the usual fourteen-week maternity leave period you do not need to give any special notice of your intention. Your employment rights should continue throughout this period, including holiday entitlement, pension rights and use of a company car. If you are self-employed you are still entitled to some kinds of benefit. Contact your Social Security Office for further details on maternity allowances.

Buying for the new baby

It has become fashionable to buy your child all the latest gear, including designer outfits and prams and pushchairs that take a rocket scientist to put together. But a great deal of this is hype and unnecessary. The baby will be quite unconcerned about the style of their vest and only concerned that it has somewhere to sleep that is comfortable. Unless you are very wealthy, you can make use of borrowed or second-hand items to save you a great deal of money. As long as you are both satisfied that the goods are safe, you can save money and avoid arguments about over-spending by being canny in your approach to equipping your nursery. Friends and family will probably have baby clothes lurking in their lofts and possibly cots and pushchairs as well. Otherwise, low-cost baby items are often advertised in newspapers, but do make sure that items bought through this route meet safety requirements.

All this planning may seem to add another stress to a life that is already busy with work and social events. But there is an important reason why you need to do this. Planning ahead will prevent you both arguing and feeling distant at a time in your lives when you need to feel close and able to work together. As a career couple, you need to face this period with a positive attitude rather than feeling as if the whole event will only be a negative time to add to your daily difficulties. It is true that, however carefully you plan, there will be surprises. Nobody can really anticipate exactly how things will work out when they first hold their new-born. Knowing that you have done your best to plan a calm beginning to this new phase of life will really help you both to maintain a secure relationship, and this is the best start you can give your baby.

The growing child

As you become used to being parents, you will face a new set of challenges. Alongside the usual concerns, like feeding and sleeping, you will both face the tricky issue of childcare arrangements. Ideally, you should have discussed this before you actually had the baby, but in the early weeks and months of parenting you may have a more realistic idea of what you think is the right way forward.

Case Study
Martina and Alan decided before their baby son was born that they would use a child-minder to care for him when Martina returned to work. They had got as far as making tentative arrangements with a recommended local child-minder when their son, Douglas, arrived. His slightly early arrival and problems with feeding put their plans out of kilter. Martina felt that she could not return to work as early as she had planned. After negotiation with her manager, she took two months more than her planned maternity leave to assure herself that Douglas would be happy with the child-minder and to resolve

some of the feeding difficulties they had encountered.

You have a number of options when deciding on appropriate childcare. Below is a summary of the various approaches you might make. Before you reach this stage, make use of the following suggestions.

- Talk through childcare issues together. Avoid a decision that is 'owned' by just one person. If you take unilateral decisions about your childcare arrangements you will set the scene for arguments about whose responsibility it is to drop off and collect the child or who should care for the child if he or she is ill. Jointly owned decisions can also help you to feel empowered about making changes if you need to.
- Make sure that you both take responsibility for safety checks about who cares for your baby. You will both know what is most important to you as well as common sense issues to check out in your child-carer (see below).
- Do not be afraid to change your mind. It is common for parents arranging childcare to feel locked into a decision once they have started down a particular road. It is OK to feel unsure about a decision and to make rearrangements. After all, it is up to you to feel satisfied that your child is receiving the best care that is available to you and them.

Different childcare arrangements

Au pairs
An au pair is really only suitable for short childcare stints because Home Office guidelines say that they should not work for more than four hours a day, totalling twenty-five hours a week. They should also not be asked to baby-sit more than two nights a week. In return they will expect board and lodging and pocket money – usually forty to fifty pounds a week. Go to a reputable au-pair agency rather than take the first girl you find. Be aware that au pairs are often inexperienced young people who probably want to learn a language as much as care for your child. Au pairs can be an

inexpensive way of finding childcare and they often develop close bonds with 'their' family, but they do have limitations and you could end up giving *them* as much care as they give your child!

Nannies

These fall into two categories: those who live with the family and those who just visit the home to provide childcare. Nannies are expensive, so you should think carefully about whether most of your hard-earned cash would go to pay for the nanny, which could defeat the object of working in the first place! Always look for a nanny through a reputable agency and double-check any references and qualifications. Call the person listed as a referee and ask them if they were satisfied with the level of care provided. Interview the nanny yourself, with your partner, and ask questions about their attitude to discipline and any other issue that concerns you. After the interview, arrange for them to meet your child. Observe how they speak to them and how the child reacts to them. Use your instincts because these can also tell you a lot about how you think the relationship might work out. Make sure you have a written contract of employment that clearly lays out any special duties, times you expect them to work and extra tasks (such as cooking the child an evening meal). Roughly speaking, a young nanny will have less experience than an older one. You might prefer a nanny who is close in age to you, or one that will be more like a grandmother figure. Without wishing to seem over-cautious, once you have engaged your nanny, try occasionally to come home at an unexpected time to check that all is as you would want it to be. Be clear about smoking and other house rules such as no sweets or only giving the baby organic food.

A relative

On the surface this arrangement has much to recommend it. You already know the person to whom you will entrust your child and they will already have a relationship with them. With a relative you can develop flexibility about dropping off and collecting your baby in a way that might not be possible in a more formal contractual agreement with a nanny or child-minder. But there are some hidden problems. You may find it more difficult to lay down particular guidelines about how you want the baby to be treated, or feel obligated to return the favour in a way that you are not happy about. It can also be difficult to pay a relative, but you could get round this by trading a task such as gardening for childcare. Many working couples do rely on relatives (mostly grandparents) to care for their children, so this is a real option when money is tight or you want to be sure that your child knows their carer well. It may also mean that you have an assurance of consistency of care as your child grows up, avoiding the swapping of one child-carer for another.

Child-minders

Child-minders are available all over the country. In the vast majority of cases you take your child to their home and they do all the same tasks that a parent would do, including feeding your baby. Most child-minders do a wonderful job but you do need to choose a child-minder very carefully. Because you are taking your child to their home, you need to be aware of all the possibilities. You do not know who comes into the home and how they behave. For instance, the child-minder herself may be a non-smoker, but her boyfriend might be a smoker. Or she may have pets you do not like. You should also consider whether you want your child to be her only charge, or whether you want a more family atmosphere with several children (child-minders are not allowed to take on more than three children at one time). Most child-minders will drop off and pick up an older child from school and will accept the child from early in the morning to the evening. *It is crucial that you find a child-minder who is on the Social Services approved list.* This means that she has had training in childcare and that her home has been vetted by a social worker. Your local Social Services hold a list of approved and registered child-minders in your area. Always pick a child-minder from this list. The Social Services may be able to advise you about typical payment to a child-minder but be careful to negotiate this before consigning your baby to them. For instance, check out whether she will charge an 'overtime' rate if you are late picking up your child.

Day nurseries and crèches

If you are lucky, one or both of you may have a work-based crèche. This can save you and your partner a great deal of effort in trying to find a reputable place to leave your child while you work. You should still apply the same rules to choosing the crèche as you would to any other childcare. Check the qualifications of the carers and the environment of the crèche. Avoid crèches that have a wide mix of age groups (unless they are separated in some way), as small children may find older children overwhelming and too demanding. You could be asked to make a financial contribution, but it will make visiting, and possibly breast-feeding, easy if necessary.

Day nurseries will often care for children from a young age but, as with other childcare arrangements, you need to pay careful attention to the qualifications of the workers and the environment they provide. Look for a variety of stimulating toys and a place where it is easy for the smaller children to be quiet. Care staff should have been properly trained in childcare and able to produce their certificates for your examination. One of the best ways to choose a nursery is by word of mouth. If your close friend recommends it and you share the same values, it may be just the place for you. Social Service departments hold lists of approved nurseries. Using an approved nursery will give you peace of mind, because the nursery will have been checked for all the things you would like to know about, but you should also ask questions for yourself.

All the above options should be reviewed and talked about as a couple. Sharing the choice of childcare can help you both to feel that you are a team and taking joint responsibility in a way that sets the scene for the future. You should also bear in mind that if the person who looks after your child, or the child themselves, is ill, or there is a family emergency, you will need contingency plans to manage caring for your child. Plan ahead what you might do in this situation and make a note of your decisions, especially if they involve other people – a relative who might stand in for a nanny, for instance. Sort out any disagreements or problems now rather than wait until a crisis strikes. No child is well all the time and having a back-up plan will help you both feel more secure.

Your relationship

The change in your relationship from being parents of a new-born to being parents of a toddler can be unnerving. Toddlers can be demanding in a different way to a small baby and may make you feel as if you are never going to have an adult conversation again. The old joke about 'Is there sex after children?' carries some truth; many couples fear that the broken nights and lack of quality time as a couple mean that intimacy disappears. Add this phenomenon to tiredness after a long day's work and you may wonder if you will ever be close again. It does not have to be like this. You can enjoy a warm and loving relationship as your child grows up. Later in the book you will find a chapter dedicated to improving and enhancing your sex life whilst living a busy lifestyle as a parent and worker. Here are some simple ideas to keep your relationship on track as you negotiate toddler territory.

Establish routines
It is strange to admit, but lots of modern couples are afraid of routines. When people mention 'routine' they tend to think slippers, cardigans and cocoa! Actually, routines are very helpful because they free you to spend time doing things that are more creative. They also build an element of predictability into a relationship. Although this is also a concept that has gone out of fashion, being predictable really only means that you can trust someone to be there for you and the family when you need him or her. With a toddler in the house, routine can save your life and partnership. Meal and bedtime routines can really help you to spend time together that is just for the two of you. A bedtime routine can be simple: evening meal, bath, story and cuddle, sleep. Be firm about giving extra drinks or watching TV until late. Just take your child back to bed and be clear about bedtime meaning bedtime. There is no need to shout or make a fuss. Remain calm and collected, but stick to your decisions. Eventually he or she will realise that you mean what you say. Praise the child when they stay in bed or sleep all night and they will gradually adapt to the routines you establish. Once they are set up you can afford to break

101

them occasionally – on your terms. Once your child is sleeping well you can begin to spend time together. Try simple things such as enjoying a take-away while watching a video, progressing to asking a trusted baby-sitter to come while you have an evening out. Always remember to give the sitter a number where you will be available or take a mobile phone with you. This kind of thing is not a luxury – it is an essential. It is at this point in your relationship that you are setting the scene for the future. If you give all your time to work or you become so child-focused that you lose your sense of what your relationship means to you both, you could end up as a divorce statistic. Your child depends upon you having a healthy relationship because it is this that will eventually give him or her the stability and confidence to go out into the world.

Enjoy each other

There is a real tendency for modern couples to view parenthood as just the 'next thing you do'. The pleasure of being in a family can get buried beneath finding the right play-school, working your way into management and rushing round the supermarket. Children (and adults) often enjoy very simple things. Try these for starters:

- Go swimming together. Not everyone enjoys swimming itself, but lots of pools now have fun areas where you can paddle or play in a fountain. Toddlers love this kind of thing and you will find that the laughter you share is worth the soggy towels and trying to dress a wriggling and wet son or daughter afterwards!
- Go for walks in the local park or countryside. If there are parks with slides and swings, so much the better. Children love to crunch through autumn leaves or throw snowballs. Walking is also very good for stress, allowing you to forget the tensions of work.
- Cook simple meals together. Rolling out pastry until it is grey, or stirring a simple cake mixture, can give a huge amount of pleasure. This is a good activity for a wet Saturday afternoon. Alternatively, use play-doh and some old pastry cutters.
- Fly kites on a picnic. Eating outside and throwing crusts for sparrows or ducks often enchants toddlers. You can also benefit

because you will see the most ordinary things in a new way through your child's eyes and this can give you an improved view of the world.

All of these ideas not only allow you to bond as a family but also give you a chance to get out of the office or factory and relax. This will lower your stress levels and help you all to avoid the tensions that can affect your relationship if all you do is work, eat and sleep. They are also relatively inexpensive and can be done at the drop of a hat. Because they may have a little more disposable income to spare, many career couples believe that they should take their children on expensive trips abroad to theme parks, particularly if friends and colleagues are doing this. The truth is that small children often enjoy very simple things and can be fazed by long journeys and strange food. It is also unhelpful to go for long periods hardly seeing your child, followed by two weeks away with your full attention. Neither you nor the child will have had the opportunity to develop a relationship and may find that it is all too much. Little and often is the best way to enjoy leisure with your family. A walk on a Sunday afternoon, or a regular bedtime story, can make all the difference to your relationship so that when the opportunity for a holiday comes along you will both be ready to get the most from it.

As a couple these issues are important because stress in your relationship with your children can put stress on your relationship with your partner, and vice versa. Having fun as a family can have a beneficial effect on you as a couple because you will see yourselves as a team with a shared goal and feel that your relationship is a success. Feeling this way will enable you to work more effectively and have somewhere to go that feels supportive if you do encounter problems at work. If you dread going home *and* feel unhappy at work, then life will seem gloomy indeed. You may find that you descend into a downward spiral, unable to lift yourself out of the difficulties. So it is worth working hard at being a family because it can nurture other areas of your life that seem, on the surface, unconnected to family life.

Teenage children

Working couples may feel that they have encountered a completely new land when their children reach their teens. The pleasant child you knew yesterday suddenly starts to sulk and shout, often over issues you regard as ridiculous. Previously content with 'own brand' trainers and T-shirts, they start demanding over-priced branded labels and shutting themselves away for hours in their bedrooms. Not only can this be stressful for your relationship with your child but it can also be hard on your relationship as a couple. Some couples find that the teens are a difficult time not only because it is hard to second-guess their son or daughter, but also because it calls to mind their own teenage years. For some couples this causes a direct comparison with the present. Individuals may remember how free and unencumbered they felt in their teens compared to their present situation with its financial and other responsibilities. Some of the tension that parents of teenagers feel can come from this source. Often it is not straight jealousy – adults know only too well the agonies of being a teenager – but more to do with a feeling that they would use all that freedom far better than their child seems to be doing. The career couple can also encounter difficulties if they expect their older child to take some responsibility around the house and find that there are many arguments over unlaid tables and washing up left in the sink. After a hard day's work, this is hardly the 'welcome home' you hope for. But you can prepare to face your teenager *and* keep your partnership intact. Here are some suggestions to help.

- Give your child a monthly allowance rather than weekly pocket money. Explain that the allowance will give them freedom to buy their own clothes and take trips out in return for certain tasks at home. These will obviously be of your own making, such as cutting the grass or hoovering, but keep the tasks within a reasonable frame. Asking for too much can mean that your child is forever failing and this is not good for their self-esteem. An allowance provides lessons in managing money and avoids a lot of arguments over spending too much on a particular item. Your child will learn that if they blow the whole lot in week one they cannot go to the cinema in week four! Of course, you will have to stick to your guns and not slip them extra cash, but this approach really can prevent a lot of problems in the long run.

- Stick together. Teenagers are masters at playing one parent off against the other. Pre-empt certain situations by discussing how you will handle them. For instance, discuss the time you expect your teenager to come home before they ask to stay out late. Agree a time and stick to it. Avoid disagreeing in front of your teenager. If you really do think that your partner has made a mistake, talk to him or her in private.
- Be understanding. Teenagers inhabit a limbo land where they want you to look after them but also to leave them alone! As a parent this can feel like riding two horses at once, with the consequent painful splitting of your heart and mind! The fact is that they are trying to make sense of a world that has little sense and do still need you to care for them. In some senses, it is no different to trying to fathom whether a baby needs a nappy change, food, drink or a cuddle when they are crying. You just have to try different approaches until you find one that works in the situation you are in at the time. The problem with teenagers is that what worked last week often does not work this week. They change so rapidly that they also find it hard to decide what they want from you. Patience and a willingness to wait for the right moment can pay off when dealing with teenagers.

All this change can mean that your relationship takes a battering. You may feel exhausted by trying to keep up and wonder where your time together disappeared. Do not give up trying to find time to be together just as a couple. This may be more difficult as your children grow up and go to bed later. Older teenagers can add another twist to this, because you may lie awake waiting for them to come home safely.

All of this can cause problems in your sex life because you may feel more observed by your teenagers and therefore have less privacy.

If your dual income allows, I would advise a weekend away occasionally. You may need to ensure that your children do not throw a wild party by suggesting they stay with friends or that a grandparent sleeps at the house, but a few days away alone can give you a chance to talk and make love in peace. These brief oases can get you through the teenage years intact and help you to feel that you do still have a relationship worth having. If weekends away are too expensive, buy a lock for your bedroom door and use it as a retreat occasionally. You may not always want to make love, but you can go there to talk or just read together – anything that helps to build your sense of closeness. Obviously I am not suggesting you lock yourself in if the third world war is raging outside, but if you want to feel private at times it can offer a small degree of security. You might also have friends who have teenagers and it can help to share some of your experiences. In this way you can feel that you are not the only one with a child who argues with everything you say or eats completely different food to everyone else in the family! But beware of breaking confidences or rubbishing your family in some way, as this can be hurtful to all of you. Having said all this about some of the problems in living with teenagers, they can bring fresh air into your family and are often full of exciting new ideas and energy that are worth having. If you work to maintain your relationship during this phase, you will benefit greatly from having enjoyed watching your children grow up. As dual workers you will also be giving your children a great model of managing work and home life. It is useful for teenagers to see and understand that life can be a rich mixture of work and leisure and if you can manage to go on enjoying good times with the family as well as working in a sensible way, you will be a good role model. The ultimate aim of a parent is to let their children out into the world equipped to make their own decisions and judgments. If you have demonstrated that this is possible in your work and family life, you will have done a good job.

About guilt

As a postscript to this chapter on children, relationships and work, I would like to add something about the most commonly encountered feeling that couples describe while trying to balance home and work life – guilt. Guilt can be felt in several different ways. For instance, Kim felt guilty that she employed a nanny to care for her baby daughter in order to return to the job as a freelance interior designer that she loved. A single parent, she felt she should be available for her baby but also felt that the best way to support them both was to work at a job she enjoyed. But when she came home and saw the nanny holding Samantha she felt guilty and sad that she could not give Samantha the full-time attention she wanted to while she was small.

One of the problems about guilt is that it is usually perceived as a negative emotion. In fact, guilt or shame can often be a potent reminder that what we are doing needs reassessment or, at the very least, reflection. In other words, because you feel guilt it does not necessarily mean that you should do the opposite of what you are currently doing, but it does mean that you need to think about what you *are* doing. For example, Kim was self-employed and realised that she had immediately gone back to the old hours of working, leaving very early in the morning and returning after 7 p.m., that she had followed prior to the birth. She decided to cut some time off her working day and be home at about 5.30 p.m. on most days. This helped her to put her guilt into perspective as well as giving her more time to play with Samantha.

Working, not working, having a child-minder or asking a relative to care for your children are all decisions you have to make to fit in with your particular lifestyles. They may not be perfect. In fact, if you took the opposite decision you might still feel guilty! If you gave up work and stayed at home you might feel guilty at not contributing to the family finances. If you work you may feel guilty at not seeing your partner enough. Every choice has an equal but opposite that contains the seeds of guilt. What the guilt can teach you is the most important element of this equation. You may never eradicate guilt completely, but that is because some guilt can be positive, reminding you of the constant need to monitor what you are doing, and why.

Some couples feel they have to be the best parents ever. They spend hours cooking organic carrots for the freezer so that they will feel less guilty about their child's diet when they are at work. Forget trying to be perfect. To steal a saying, 'Life is too short to stuff a mushroom'! Use the time-saving opportunities open to you. Supermarkets are full of convenience foods that you can use to save precious time. If you must spend hours in the kitchen, make it an indulgence rather than a chore, unless kneading dough helps to beat your stress levels. As long as you follow a reasonably healthy diet, the odd frozen pizza eaten in front of the TV will not kill you. If you must feel guilty, feel guilty about spending too long at the office and not seeing your partner, or spending yet another Saturday hunched over your PC. Feeling guilty about not serving cordon bleu food, or not buying your child designer dungarees, is wasted emotion.

Next time you feel guilty, try the following:

- Ask yourself about the source of the guilt. Is it something you know you need to change but have put off? If this is the case, resolve to take action rather than prevaricate. Take a day off or give yourself an early finish to the day and deal with whatever you feel uncomfortable about.

- Talk to your partner about your feelings. If you cannot take immediate action, promise to deal with the issue later. For instance, Rosemary had to undertake a lengthy report for her department. It would mean long hours and at least one weekend working on the information. She explained how guilty she felt that the work would spoil her partner's birthday. She told him that she would take some holiday leave after the report was finished and they could go away for a break.

- Chronic guilt is a sign that you have allowed a situation to build up without taking positive action, perhaps because it is not immediately obvious what the action should be. Try writing your feelings down. It does not matter what order you write them in.

Use your notes to look at the feelings you have generated. Sometimes your inability to act will be obviously linked to a particular set of feelings. Now think about positive actions that could alleviate some of the difficult feelings. Pick one or two of these and try out your ideas. It does not matter if they are not perfect solutions, because new ways of doing things often take several attempts to get right. You will have started on the path to dealing with your guilt.

Case Study

Una felt a vague and nagging sense of guilt about her husband Richard. Because of this she found herself trying to hide how much she enjoyed work, often joining in when he moaned about his job and remaining quiet about the fun she had as a retail assistant. She knew she was not being honest about her pleasure at work, but felt it would be somehow disloyal to tell Richard how much she looked forward to it. One day Richard was telling Una again how bored he was with his job in IT and how much he wanted to work at a nearby firm which had more interesting computer systems. Una suddenly blurted out that he should 'stop whingeing and try for a job there'. Richard was stunned. He had assumed that Una also found work a boring necessity. At first he was upset, but after a short while he asked Una why she had spoken out. Una explained that she had felt guilty about enjoying her work and how much fun she had with her colleagues. Richard realised that Una had a quality of work that he envied and was spurred on to try for a post at the firm that interested him. He was eventually successful in getting a job.

Una and Richard made an interesting discovery. Guilt can sometimes freeze individuals and couples in situations where they feel uncomfortable, rather than allowing them to make the changes they need. In other words, Una's feelings of guilt and her silence about her own happy situation, did not help Richard feel better about work. In fact, they made things worse because Richard thought that everybody, including Una, felt bored at work. If Una had examined her feelings of guilt and asked herself why she was acting in a way that was actually a deception, Richard might have been able to make a change more quickly.

Guilt, then, is not a wasted feeling. It can really spur you on to make changes to concerns that you know are not as they ought to be. Never to feel guilty might be interpreted as being insensitive and out of touch with others. It is very hard to feel guilty about a situation you do not care about, so you could see guilt as a 'tap on the shoulder', reminding you that, because you care, you should take some action that allows you to make reparation. But guilt is not usually settled with gifts and expensive holidays. Most people really know that buying their daughter an expensive toy is not as good as deciding not to spend so much time at work in the future. To really put guilt in its place you will probably have to make a personal decision that may even be emotionally costly – but it will be worth it.

Chapter review

This chapter has been about children, work and relationships. Each section dealt with a different aspect of parenting and work. The challenges of children at different ages were explored and practical information and suggestions offered about managing the change that children bring to a career couple. The last part of the chapter looked at guilt and how this can be handled effectively, especially in respect to family life.

5

Keeping your love life alive when you both work

The working couple can often feel that they are besieged by life – paying bills, organising childcare, delivering deadlines at work and maintaining family life. With all this on their mind it is no wonder that sex can become a chore rather than a pleasure. Often relegated to the end of the day and after a heavy day at work, sex can seem like another deadline to be met rather than an expression of love between two partners. Too often couples feel guilt at not having sex as often as they imagine everyone else is, but also resentful at the time and effort that sex requires when they are already tired. The good news is that your sexual relationship does not have to be like this. You *can* enjoy a sex life that is not lacklustre and boring.

Putting the passion back into sex can be simple, but it requires willingness from both of you to want to enjoy sex again. This may sound an odd thing to say, but sometimes one partner may resist working on restoring their sex life because they think it will threaten the status quo in the relationship. They may fear change because it will bring increased responsibilities. They may wonder if they can cope with any extra load on top of an already stressed lifestyle. But sex can be a great stress reliever, both from an emotional and physical point of view. Far from adding to stress, a good sex life can provide a break from the tensions of everyday life.

Common reasons for sexual problems

- For most career couples, the problem that tops the list as a cause of sexual problems is tiredness. Many couples find themselves exhausted after a day at work and looking after the family in the evening. Often this is not a physical exhaustion (although looking after small children can be physically exhausting), but a mental exhaustion that seems to leave little room for intimacy. This kind of tiredness can cause individuals to want to slump down in front of the TV or to knock back a bottle of wine in order to switch off. It is no wonder that when the couple finally gets to bed sex is no longer on the agenda.

- Problems that 'leak' into your sex life from other areas of your life can wreck your closeness to one another. For instance, Matthew had a difficult relationship with his line manager. She appeared to be very erratic in the way that she managed her staff. One day would be good, with little or no tension, the next would be full of her anger and criticism so that the staff felt under pressure and often confided in Matthew. Matthew felt permanently on edge, and was often so restless he could not sleep because of facing his manager the next day. Matthew and Helen, his wife, noticed that their sex life had diminished to almost nothing because Matthew was so taken up with his work problem. 'Switching off' cares and worries can be tough and requires a special effort if it is to succeed.

- Personal problems that have not been dealt with can attack your relationship and undermine your sexual response to one another. Feelings of anger, sadness or a lack of trust can all undermine how you respond to each other in bed and develop into a downward spiral of coldness towards one another. This is exacerbated by an inability to sort out the underlying problem and so the couple can face not only sexual problems but also difficulties in general communication.

- Change in the family can lead to sexual problems. Concerns such as bereavement, illness, job loss, caring for an elderly relative and many others, can prevent a couple from enjoying sex. To some extent this is a natural response to difficult times, but if it drags on for several months it may cause the couple to feel awkward about resuming their sex life.

- The arrival of children can upset a couple's sexual response to each other. This is so common that many mothers and fathers joke about the lack of sex in the early years of parenthood! Not only does the mother have to cope with the physical changes to her body, including possible stitches to a tear or an episiotomy after childbirth and sore breasts from breast-feeding, but there are broken nights and the presence of the baby in the parents' room to contend with. Added to this are the psychological changes that a new baby brings to most couples as they face up to the responsibilities of parenting. This is sometimes described as 'mummying and daddying' the partnership. All this really means is that couples can lose sight of one another as sexual adults, seeing themselves as 'mummy' or 'daddy' instead. This can often take some time to get over after the new baby arrives.

Common myths about sex

Everybody is having sex all the time. It is just us that do not have a regular sex life

This is an old chestnut of a myth that seems to afflict lots of couples. The truth is that the average amount of sex that most people have is less than the media would lead us to believe. The 1994 survey of the sexual behaviour of over 20,000 people demonstrates that even in their early twenties (traditionally the most sexually active period) the average number of times people had sexual intercourse was 4 to

5 times a month. The average drops for people in their thirties and forties and then reaches a plateau for people in older age groups. So the idea that everybody is at it like knives is simply untrue! Remember, these figures represent an average, so it means that while there were some people who had sex more frequently there were plenty who had sex much less than the average. You are not alone.

Everybody else has sexual desire that remains constant. I am the only one who experiences ups and downs in desire

This myth may have originated in the almost omnipresent media attention to sex all around us. Every poster, newspaper and magazine has sexually provocative material in it – from Wonderbra advertising to topless models in the *Sun* – and we seem to have accepted the notion that we are all switched on, ready for sex the moment it is available. This is simply not true. Most people in a committed relationship experience sexual desire as 'waxing and waning'. They may make love three times one week (or in one night!) and then not make love again for two weeks. Some couples go months without intercourse and then enjoy a period of intense love-making. Whatever pattern is right for you is OK. Other issues can also affect your desire. For instance, you may just be getting over a bad bout of flu, had a row about the electricity bill or be worried about your mother who is in hospital. Nobody is really a sex machine, just waiting to have the right button pushed to want sex. We are complex organisms who are affected by what is going on around us and how we feel about these events, at any given moment.

Sex should be spontaneous. We should know when we both want to make love without talking about it openly

This myth is probably responsible for more missed love-making opportunities than any other. The idea that you do not need to talk about and plan for love-making is unrealistic. It stems from the old idea that two lovers should be able to look into each other's eyes and read their minds. This is not entirely fanciful, because some lovers do experience something like this at the beginning of their relationship, but this soon fades. To conduct an adult relationship you need to be able to talk about difficult issues as well as those where you naturally agree. Sex requires conversation and a sharing of likes and dislikes, pleasures and pains. This is especially true if you are unwell or new parents. Expecting your partner to know how you feel without talking in these circumstances can end in tears. Imagine applying the non-talking rule to another human appetite – eating. How would you know when your partner was hungry? How could you share your need to eat? And how could you explain you hate sprouts but like carrots? Sex is no different. You need to communicate mutual desires and whether you feel like a banquet or a snack! Learning to talk like this can stand you in good stead for the future, because you will be able to negotiate when change affects your relationship without hoping your partner spots the signs of discontent by ESP.

If you have to try to feel interested in sex you might as well not bother to go any further. It might even be a sign that the relationship is over

This myth is a variation on the previous one and seems to have its roots in the idea that sexual desire should well up from inside the moment you are with your partner. This is not the experience of couples in real relationships. It is not unusual for a busy lifestyle to push sexual desire underground so that the couple needs to work to uncover desire and restore sexual interest. This is rather like the feeling that some people have when they are working hard and forget to eat. Many people in this situation say something like 'Well, I felt hungry earlier, but I've got past the need now'. Sometimes the desire to eat returns as the person relaxes. Sex can be similar. The desire for sex can reawaken when the circumstances are right, so that 'trying' to enjoy sex might just mean finding a way to relax or break a boring routine. Sexual difficulties are rarely a sign that the relationship is over. But they can act as a barometer to indicate that the relationship needs some attention. Simple steps, rather than a separation, can solve many sexual problems. In fact, there is evidence from Relate (the couple counselling charity) that healing sexual problems can have a knock-on positive effect on more general relationship difficulties, such as communication problems.

Once you have made a commitment to someone, sex loses all passion.
It becomes a routine and you should not expect anything else
The variety and passion that married couples and long-term co-
habitees experience in their sex lives is a well-kept secret. We are so
used to reading about sex and young, single people, and associating
the hype surrounding celebrities and stars with passion, that the
idea that the ordinary couple you passed on the street yesterday
might enjoy a passionate love life has become almost a joke. The
truth is that lots of long-term couples enjoy a happy and exciting sex
life – they just do not talk about it to others very often. It is also true
that couples can get into a rut in their sex lives, going through the
same routines and making love at the same times each week. This
often happens when couples are very busy or fail to prioritise love-
making. Lack of love-making may be due to a busy lifestyle, but can
also be due to a lack of satisfaction with sex because it is too fast,
unarousing or lacking in sensitivity. As in many different situations
in relationships, sex needs good communication if it is to succeed.

Improving your sex life

Wander into your local stationers and it is not unusual to find whole
magazines devoted to sexual technique. Twenty years ago, only the
'top shelf' magazines would have any frank sexual content. Nowadays
most women's and many men's magazines have explicit information
about sex. It can all sound complicated and specialised and also aimed
at people who seem to live very different lifestyles to the ordinary
person. But it does not have to be complicated to improve your sex
life. Follow the ideas below to help you take some first steps to
improve your sex life.

Prioritise sex

In the same way that you book time at the hairdresser, gym and squash club, book time for sex. Earlier in the book I suggested that you block part of your diary so that you can spend time together. This works well for sex, but it means not only booking potential work time but also time that you might have spent socialising at evenings and weekends. Make a note in your diary and treat it like a date. The argument against this kind of approach is that it is too 'clinical' and 'planned'. This is not really an argument that holds water. Thousands of people spend a great deal of time on a Saturday thinking about their date with their girlfriend or boyfriend, often planning to spend the night together and make love. Nobody suggests that this is calculating or boring. In fact, the 'getting ready' time is often extremely exciting and arousing. Couples in a committed partnership can revive some of this spirit in looking forward to love-making.

Case Study

Maddy and Josh had met through a works evening out and were very attracted to each other. Eventually they moved in together and enjoyed a fulfilling sex life for two years. As their relationship matured, Maddy felt that Josh was less interested in making love. They spent a lot of time with their friends, meeting them each Friday and Saturday at the local pub. Because they had moved into an old house, they also spent a great deal of time decorating and gardening, creating the perfect house for the two of them. The lack of sex began to worry Maddy. She wondered if Josh had lost interest in her or if he was seeing someone else. Eventually she tackled him about their sex life. Josh did not really know what to say to Maddy, but tried to explain how tired he often felt and that sex was often the last thing on his mind at the end of the day. Maddy and Josh puzzled over why this had happened to them. After all, they had previously enjoyed a good sex life. Maddy found herself talking to Josh about the early days of their relationship when they had spent whole days in bed, talking and making love. Josh remembered racing home from work to dive into the shower before meeting Maddy. Maddy and Josh slowly realised that this lazy and relaxed sex had vanished as they had thrown themselves into their house and begun a hectic round of socialising. They decided to recreate the beginning of their partnership the next Saturday. They began by cancelling arrangements to meet the other couples they usually met and put the paint pots away. When Saturday came, they spent the whole day in bed together, sharing jokes and favourite food as well as making love. Josh and Maddy felt completely different and promised each other that they would take steps to cut down outside interests and spend more quality time together. They made sure this would not just be a promise, but would also happen in reality by writing their 'dates' in their diary.

Maddy and Josh made a discovery to which many other couples can bear witness: feelings about sex and love-making can often return once time is given to approaching sex when the couple are not tired and unable to respond. Making time to be together is also important because talking about sex usually requires understanding and sensitivity towards your partner. It is hard to develop this understanding if you are rushed into sex and anxious to get it over because you want to go to sleep.

Reflect on what you actually do together

You might imagine that I am about to launch into a diatribe about sexual technique, encouraging you to learn the *Karma Sutra* or *The Joy of Sex* off by heart! But I am actually going to suggest the opposite. You may have read all the sex manuals and feel you know all the positions that exist, but this may not have helped you to enjoy sex and to feel free about enjoying it as a shared pleasure. In fact, you may be haunted by the 'sex police', imagining that you must make love in the way that couples in films and books seem to. This is the Curse of James Bond – the idea that sex is always earth moving and never needs a condom! As a committed couple you will know that sex rarely lives up to this. Yes, you will have earth-moving moments, but often sex is comforting, fun, and warm or more like an extended cuddle than multi-orgasmic. This is natural and is what happens between most couples as they grow to know and feel closer to their partner. The great secret is that you do not always have to have full intercourse. Sometimes you can enjoy a sensual cuddle, a massage, a talk that includes caressing and stroking or stimulation of your partner or yourself that does not include penetration. You may well have done all these things when you were going out together, but become hooked into full sex as the 'right' thing to do now you are a couple in the eyes of the world. If you are busy and tired, these alternatives to intercourse can allow you to be close and affectionate rather than constantly waiting for the perfect moment to make love. Expressing your feelings for each other can then take a varied style to suit your mood and circumstances.

Case Study

Nina and Don had been married for four years when they admitted to each other that sex lacked the sparkle it had had in the early years of their marriage. Both had been promoted in the local government office where they worked and led extremely busy lives, often working at weekends. They had, however, managed to carry on making love, but it always seemed to be in the same style and on the same day – Friday evenings. Nina told Don that she felt she wanted more touching and kissing, while Don wanted to slow down the whole event. Once they had braved the discussion they tried out different ways of enjoying sex over the next few weeks. Nina felt they were far more tender towards each other and that this improved their daily life as well. Don and Nina laughed a lot in bed and enjoyed 'messing about', as they termed it, instead of going straight to intercourse.

Nina and Don not only prioritised their love-making but were also able to reduce the tension that had previously seemed to accompany their sex life. This can happen when couples are open to new ways of being sexual together. Experimenting with different expressions of sexual feelings can also help a couple if they encounter a period of change. For instance, new parents may welcome alternatives to full intercourse as they resume their sex life after the birth of their child. Illness, personal problems and a temporary imbalance of desire can all be helped by sharing sex that is right for the moment and situation rather than feeling that there is only one correct way to have a sex life. Learn to trust your instincts and intuition about what seems right for your relationship rather than punish yourself because you do not have sex in the way you think everybody else does. Break away from the idea that sex has to be all or nothing and you may find that you enjoy it much more.

Relax into love-making

Relaxation is the key to enjoying and wanting sex. The most common cause of lack of sexual desire is tension. Chronic stress can gradually eat away at sexual desire until it disappears altogether. You may wonder how you can find time to relax but there are some easy steps to take that can help you to relax. You should try to include these ideas and exercises whether you want to make love or not. Let them become a regular part of your lifestyle and you will notice the difference.

- *Watch less TV*
  The temptation to flop down in front of the set at the end of the day can be overpowering, but TV can actually wind you up rather than soothe you. Try playing gentle music or alternatively any music that you know helps you to feel less tense. If you want to play 'home disco' and dance around as well, this can also help you to feel less wound up!

- *Take more exercise*
  You do not have to join a gym, but an evening walk or a little weekend gardening (do not overdo this, because strained backs are not conducive to relaxing) can help you to feel better about yourself. Exercise releases endorphins – the body's natural relaxant.

- *Practise breathing more slowly*
This is a good exercise to try in the office or at home. Slow breathing can be deeply relaxing, allowing you to work at home or at your job feeling less tense. It is also unobtrusive and can be practised during a lunch break or at home while listening to music. First of all, close your eyes and breathe in a normal way for a minute or so. Now take in a breath through your nose, hold, and then release through the mouth. Count three for each stage – in, two, three; hold, two, three; out, two, three. Follow this pattern for three or four minutes. As you release the breath, try to imagine you are breathing out all your tension. Follow the breathing pattern until you are ready to return to normal breathing. You should notice that your muscles have also relaxed and that you feel less stressed. A few breaths of this kind, without closing your eyes, can also help to dispel nerves – especially before a speech or presentation. They can sometimes divert a headache if you can catch it before it gets too firmly established. Learning to control tension in this way can pay dividends. You are much less likely to take concerns home with you if you can let go of tension, and will therefore feel more disposed to enjoy sex.

- *Eat properly*
At the risk of sounding too much like your mother, you need to pay attention to what you eat and when you eat it. Skipping meals and eating junk food can leave you feeling uncomfortable and uninterested in sex. Irregular eating lowers blood sugar and can cause feelings of depression and headaches, including migraine. It is important to eat a good breakfast – cereal and wholemeal toast is ideal. Fried breakfasts can carry a great deal of fat which the body finds hard to break down. During the day, eating little and often can help to reduce the blood sugar slump that leads to tension and stress. Avoid processed foods – cakes, biscuits and chocolate – and eat fruit and carbohydrates that will help you feel full but not produce a sugar peak that is swiftly followed by a stress-inducing dip. Try replacing coffee with herbal tea or decaffeinated coffee. Coffee may help to keep you going through the

day, but it can wind you up so much that you find relaxing difficult to achieve and sex hard to focus on.

- *Dispense with false stimulants*
  Alcohol can produce a false feeling of relaxation and should be kept to a minimum – not more than a glass or two of wine a day, a pint of beer or a shot of spirits. Cut out cannabis and other so-called 'recreational' drugs that will not only wreck your sex life, but also your career and other relationships. Smoking has a proven track record of causing sexual problems in men and may well have a similar effect on women. Whatever the cause, smoking is a form of addiction and produces a feeling of relaxation that is only the body's response to receiving a 'fix'. Giving up smoking will not only do your health good but also make you much nicer to kiss and be close to. As the advert once said 'Who wants to kiss an ashtray?' Learning to be close to your partner without false stimulants can give you a natural 'high' that is much more satisfying than the things you may try to help you relax.

- *Follow your dreams*
  Most people have a dream that they would like to bring to fruition, but do not know how to make happen. Spend some time daydreaming about what you want. It may be that you have always hankered after a house by the sea or to write a novel. It does not matter too much what you dream about. It may be achievable or it may be slightly off-beam. Whatever your dream, allow yourself to speculate about how it could happen. Sometimes dreams can bring forward new ideas and thoughts that help us to feel interested in life and renew our sense of purpose. This can nurture our relationships and our sex lives, especially if your partner shares your dreams. Play with the ideas a little because they probably represent the creative side of you that is also present in sex. Sex, after all, is a type of play that adults can enjoy. Apply a little of this to your dreams and sex life and you will find that relaxation and sex can become fun again.

Communicate about your sex life

It is strange but true that many couples, perhaps the majority, find talking about sex very difficult. This is probably due to the cliché that talking about sex means that the relationship is no longer spontaneous and that this sounds the death knell for successful intimacy. As you have discovered earlier in this chapter, this is a misunderstanding about real partnerships. In order to maintain a good sex life you need to be able to share your thoughts and desires rather than hope your partner can guess what you like or dislike. Follow the pointers below in order to discuss sex successfully.

- *Be positive – avoid talking about sex in a negative way*
  For example, Penny did not like it when Pat handled her breasts roughly during sex. She and Pat often stopped in the act because Penny had said something like 'You're doing it again. How many times do I have to tell you about grabbing me like that?' This kind of outburst often meant that they stopped making love and then did not speak to each other for a day or two. Penny had never handled it any other way, chiefly because she hoped that it would be obvious to Pat what she really wanted, which was gentle stroking and caressing. Pat felt rebuffed and unsure of what he was supposed to do. As far as he was concerned he was not deliberately being rough, but responding with passion. A better approach to letting your partner know what you want is to frame your discussions in a positive way. For instance, Penny could have said something like 'I find it very arousing when you stroke my breasts in a sensuous way'. Pat would have immediately understood what she wanted and the row could have been avoided. Sometimes this positive way of explaining something can be enhanced by demonstrating what you want. Penny might have taken Pat's hand and showed him what she wanted to happen. Adopting a positive approach to communicating with your partner about sex can also help you to think about what you do enjoy.

- **Change where you talk about sex**

If you have experienced problems in talking about sex in the past, try changing the venue where you talk about it. For example, if you have often had rows about sex in the bedroom, try initiating your discussions in the lounge. Distancing your discussions from love-making can sometimes be helpful because psychologically you are no longer in the 'argument zone' (this can be helpful for other kinds of arguments too). Ensure that you will be uninterrupted and then start by saying something like 'I feel that I would like to talk about our sex life . . .' You can then carry on by outlining your difficulties or suggestions. Make sure you build in plenty of pauses so that your partner can add their own observations, and ask them open questions such as 'How do you feel about the frequency of our love-making?' This approach leaves plenty of space for your partner to respond, rather than using a closed question that can evoke a one-word answer. An example of a closed question is 'You do agree with me about the frequency of our love-making, don't you?' There are really only two answers to a closed question – yes or no. Using this kind of question will virtually guarantee that you will never find out what your partner really thinks or feels.

- **Use language you are comfortable with**

When talking about sex with a partner it is OK to use the pet names you may have for each other. For example, Beth always referred to her partner's penis as 'Harry' because of a personal joke they had shared years before. If this kind of nickname is comfortable for you, use it when you talk to each other. The only place where this is not a good idea is where it might cause confusion and make it difficult for your partner to understand exactly what you are asking for or commenting on. In these situations, use the names that describe the part of the body you are referring to – penis, vagina, clitoris etc. Be wary of using base terms to describe your partner. You may feel that calling your partner's penis a 'prick' or 'todger' is affectionate, but they may not view it in the same way. Unless you are very sure that they are OK with this, stick to the usual names for genitals.

- *Listen carefully to your partner's point of view*
  As in all discussions, it is important to listen and absorb what your partner has to say. Talking about sex can often elucidate a defensive response because of the embarrassment factor that many people experience when discussing sex. Listening and attending can help to reduce the embarrassment that you may both feel. If you listen attentively you can pick up what is not said as well as what your partner is saying. Watch for a lack of eye contact, long pauses before speaking and words that are stumbled on. All these can indicate that the speaker is having trouble saying exactly what they wanted to say, or are trying not to hurt your feelings. It is also useful to reflect back on what your partner has said so that they can be sure you have really understood them. Here is a typical conversation between Kevin and his partner Mary.

Kevin: "When we make love I think you concentrate too much on direct stimulation of my penis. Although I do enjoy this, I want you to caress me all over and to stimulate me later on in our lovemaking rather than straight away."

Mary reflects back: "I think you are asking me to slow down on direct stimulation of your penis and to caress the whole of your body during lovemaking."

This may sound a slightly laborious way of communicating, but it can prevent unhelpful assumptions and ensure that effective listening is actually taking place. If you practise this mode of talking for a few months you will find it seems less strange and becomes part of your normal way of talking to one another. If your partner has not understood what you have been trying to say, and this is clear from their reflection, try repeating what you have been trying to explain in a slightly different way. It is important to remain calm while talking and to avoid sarcasm and cynical remarks. Saying 'Yes, well that's going to happen' in a sarcastic style will only put a barrier between you and your partner. Most sarcasm is the product of fear and defensiveness, so if you find you use it a lot you need to examine why you may be finding it hard to be open to new ideas.

Improve your self-confidence about your body

Many people feel self-conscious about their bodies. Fashion has always influenced our view of what is attractive and what is not. No doubt there were women in Rubens' time who bemoaned the fact that they were just not plump enough! The problem is that for every person who fits the current fashions there are thousands more who are not these so-called regulation shapes. The idea that they are not slim enough, muscular enough, tall enough or tanned enough has blighted the sex lives of many people. As a psychosexual therapist I have met many people who feel that they must avoid being seen naked because they fear their partner will hate their body. They cover themselves with sheets or insist on having the light off. Sometimes the dislike applies to only one part of their body. They hate their thighs or chest. Some resort to moving as little as possible during sex to prevent a partner seeing their 'faulty' body. This kind of behaviour and self-loathing can ruin a sexual relationship. To overcome this problem you need to see yourself in a different light. If you live in as healthy a way as you can, with a sensible diet and reasonable exercise, you have a body that is yours and needs accepting. Often, problems with body image are not due to a real problem with big thighs or small pecs, but to a fear that comes from within and this is usually a fear of rejection. We all suffer from this to a greater or lesser extent. Remember how you felt on your first day at work, at school or on your first date. The anxiety that we will not be thought intelligent or attractive can be overwhelming and frightening. This is the same feeling that some individuals experience when they worry that a partner will not like their body. It can occur at any point in a partnership – often after a significant change such as childbirth or illness.

To restore your sense of caring for your body try the following ideas:

- **When bathing or showering run your hands over your body**
  Use oils or shower-gel and enjoy the smoothness of your skin. Stop yourself focusing on areas you disapprove of. Instead, enjoy the sensuous quality of the warm water on your body.

- **Ask your partner to play a game with you**
  Ask him or her to name his or her favourite part of your body and then do the same for them. Carry on until you run out of places! Be prepared to accept the compliments instead of brushing them aside.

- **Buy the most expensive grooming aids you can afford**
  Even if you cannot do this every week, save up for a treat every so often. A favourite perfume or aftershave can help you feel a million dollars. Wear clothes you like and feel good in. This is *not* the same as buying ultra-fashionable clothes, because these can sometimes make you feel worse about yourself. Most people have a style that they feel suits them. Following this can improve your self-esteem.

- **Enter into the sensations of sex**
  Some people feel as if they are having an 'out of body' experience when they have sex because they are so busy wondering whether they look OK and are doing it right, trying not to see their own body or trying to adjust their position to hide the part they do not want their partner to see. In fact, they might as well not be making love at all! Instead of all these manoeuvrings, allow yourself to feel the softness of your partner's touch, their breath on your skin, the warmth in the room and the flickering of the candles. In fact, focus on anything that is pleasurable rather than stress inducing. Allow yourself to wallow in the arousal process and your body will become a conduit to enjoyment rather than a wall that prevents you from feeling sexy.

- *Try a form of exercise that allows you to feel in touch with your body*
  Exercise can help you to feel more comfortable about your body by familiarising you with its shape and abilities. Choose an exercise that is body-friendly – yoga, for example – rather than an exercise regime that exhausts you and causes you to want to subdue your body – such as tough aerobics. That said, some people enjoy the 'high' that aerobic exercise can give and this can be very body affirming in some circumstances. It is really a matter of seeking the right thing that suits you and helps you to know your own body well. Gentle exercise or exercise that allows you to get to know the way your body functions is helpful. Exercise that you take because you hate your body and want it to 'behave' runs the risk of alienating you further from your sensuous side. This is also true of dieting. If you feel uncomfortable about your weight, it is right to take action. But avoid the kind of diet that crushes your spirit. Take proper advice about dieting and avoid crash diets that set up a 'yo-yo' effect where you lose and then gain weight in a descending spiral.

Practical help for love-making

Here are some simple ideas that can make a huge difference to enjoying sex. Alternate the ideas so that you build in novelty and interest and avoid the routines that many people feel they fall into when making love.

- *Set the scene*
  Create a space that is pleasant to make love in. If you only ever make love in the bedroom on crumpled sheets, setting the scene for sex can help you feel more positive about it. Make sure the room you choose is warm and comfortable and has low lighting. Candles are great – they are flattering and romantic. Scented candles can also help, especially those with a musky scent. Clean, cool, cotton sheets can be a turn-on, as can silky bed clothes, but a smoothed-

out duvet can also be alluring. You might also try dragging the duvet into another room – perhaps the lounge – or draping it on a sofa.

- **Set the mood**
  In every good romance film, as the lovers kiss, the orchestra in the background strikes up a passionate piece of music. Music can powerfully influence sexual mood and can be extremely helpful in love-making. Choose music that has a personal meaning, such as the piece that was playing the night you met, classical music that has soaring passages, such as the Elgar Cello Concerto, or raunchy rock music that has a good bass rhythm. Avoid complex modern music that has too much dissonance or music that has any powerful associations you would rather avoid. You might also try the now widely available CDs and tapes with natural sounds such as waves on a beach or forest sounds. Use your imagination and find music that could be a personal soundtrack to your love-making. Make sure that you remove other distractions such as a TV or radio on in another room.

- **Set yourself up**
  If you have planned to make love, get ready for love-making in the same way that you might get ready for a date. Bath or shower and wash your hair. Use oils and perfume if you usually do and apply a little light make-up if you want to. Some people are happy to start love-making naked, but you can have fun in undressing. Choose your clothes with care. You may want to wear everyday clothes with no underwear, special lingerie you have bought for the occasion or go the whole hog and wear a fantasy outfit you know your partner (and you) would enjoy. Silky boxer shorts or thong knickers can be sexy, but you must find clothes that you feel OK about wearing. It will not help you to feel ready for love-making if you are wearing something your partner chose but you hate. Above all, you must feel comfortable in what you wear, so explain why you hate push-up bras or tight jeans before you get to sex. Having a row in the middle of sex will ruin the moment and the resulting tension could last for days.

- **Set your imagination**

The question of fantasy in love-making is controversial. Some people feel it is a useful tool that does no harm. Others feel it is a betrayal of their partner. But there are different forms of fantasy. It can be beneficial if used in a particular way. For instance, fantasising during love-making does not just mean thinking about another person. You might imagine you are lying on a beach with the warm sand on your back and the sea brushing your toes, or in a meadow with the grass waving over your head. Some people fantasise about making love in a public place – a lift between floors or a local park. This 'venue' fantasising can be arousing and does not involve thinking about other people at all. For those who believe that fantasising about people is harmless (as long as it stays a fantasy), imagining the hands of another caressing them is exciting and adds to the passion. This kind of fantasy can involve faceless people rather than imagining your neighbour having sex with you. Be wary about focusing on a particular person too often, as this can cause a kind of emotional block that can be hard to break. Fantasising about film or pop stars is probably harmless if it just adds a sparkle to love-making rather than providing an escape from a sexual experience you are not enjoying. Fantasising to escape indicates that there is a problem with your sex life that needs addressing, not running away from.

- **Set your feelings**

One of the most frequent problems that couples encounter is in trying to move from everyday life to sex. One moment you may be changing a nappy or driving home from work, the next trying to feel in the mood for love-making. This can be a real obstacle to love-making, but you can overcome the problem by allowing yourselves enough time to feel close to your partner before moving to sex. Allow at least an extra hour if you have been caught up in work issues or home life. You may find that changing clothes or bathing will buy some of this time, but you can use the hour to good effect. Avoid talking about work and office politics. Instead, be affectionate. Share a glass of wine (but only one or your sex plans may have to be put on hold!) and cuddle and kiss each other as you unwind. In fact, being affectionate is an underrated skill. Affection is the oil on the wheels of a relationship, so build affection in to daily life. A hug or kiss, kind word or thoughtful action can all improve a relationship and pave the way for a successful sexual relationship because the couple have a pathway to closeness already well established. Lack of affection can mean that the relationship has wandered into a serious problem. In fact, lack of sex is less serious than lack of affection because the couple may feel estranged from each other through lack of affection, whereas lack of sex may be due to a temporary problem – such as recovery from an illness, for instance.

Common sexual problems encountered by career couples

Working couples often encounter specific sexual difficulties that spoil their sex lives. These problems can seem unconnected to other parts of life and come out of the blue. In other situations, the problem can appear to be just one of many difficulties. The following problems are much more common than people imagine, and can be experienced by people of any age.

Loss of desire

Statistics from Relate, the couple counselling charity, indicate that loss of desire is *the* number one sexual problem that couples encounter. Forty per cent of women told Relate psychosexual therapists that this was their chief problem and the difficulty has doubled in men approaching Relate in recent years. Loss or lack of desire is linked to other issues that the busy working couple know only too well – tiredness, stress and anxiety all have a negative affect on libido. Taking action to diminish stress and tiredness can improve libido, but this may not be enough. Loss of desire may also occur because of a lack of personal self-esteem, and it is this that needs working on.

If you have suffered a disappointment at work or argued a great deal at home, your self-esteem will have taken a battering. You can help to switch off negative thoughts about yourself by listing all the things you have achieved or feel proud of.

Case Study

Lucy felt that her self-esteem had plummeted since leaving work. She had been ill for several months with a virus that kept returning and was advised by her GP to cut her work hours. Her firm reacted by telling her that this was not possible – she had to work full time or not at all. Lucy chose to leave, but felt miserable about this. As a result of the illness and loss of work, her sexual desire had deserted her. Dan, her boyfriend, helped her to make a list that outlined her abilities.

- Mother to eight-year-old Tanya (her child by a former relationship). Tanya was happy and doing well at school, with a talent for singing that meant she had a starring role in the school play.
- Had completed a course of study a year earlier which led to a Certificate in Computer Studies.
- A good cook – especially of puddings and cakes that all her friends enjoyed.
- A thoughtful girlfriend who had supported Dan when he had moved jobs recently.
- A good listener – the kind of person that others turned to when in trouble or unhappy. Dan suggested that this could be the basis of a new career because people often remarked on it.
- Affectionate and kind partner who normally enjoyed love-making.

When Lucy read what they had written together she realised that she still had a lot going for her and felt better about herself. Dan also encouraged her to feel sensual by giving her massages with scented massage oil and performing intimate tasks such as washing and brushing Lucy's hair.

Desire can also be reawakened by more direct means. Intimate touching and cuddling which does not go on to intercourse can eventually help you feel more able to respond sexually, although you may need to instigate regular 'sessions' over a month or six weeks. Watching sexy films can help, but I would advise against using soft or hard porn because the images can be too intrusive, and degrading rather than arousing. You might be more helped by watching a lovers' guide video or buying a sex manual to help you explore your own sexuality, but be wary of forcing yourself to do this if you feel you are doing it only to please your partner rather than yourself. Lastly, you may find that masturbation can help you to feel a sense of desire again. If you have stopped making love, your desire may have gone underground rather than disappeared. Stroking yourself in the bath or bed, and enjoying the consequent sensations of arousal can bring your feelings of desire back to the surface. Again, you may need to do this for a few weeks to notice a difference.

Loss of libido, especially in women, can also be triggered by hormonal changes. The menopause and other menstrual disturbances can affect women's sexual feelings. A visit to your GP could help you to understand why your desire has changed. Do not forget to check out the effect of taking the contraceptive Pill or other medicines that can affect libido – such as some anti-depressants.

Loss of libido may also be a symptom of greater problems in the relationship. If you feel you cannot trust your partner or that you have drifted apart, your loss of desire may be a protective psychological effect, occurring because you do not want to risk further emotional pain. If this seems likely, you could benefit from seeing a couple counsellor or psychosexual therapist (see contacts in the back of the book). Couple counselling or therapy for sexual desire and relationship difficulties can be extremely helpful. Relate statistics demonstrate that over 75 per cent of couples rated therapy as improving their relationship so that it was 'now as I want it to be'. Psychosexual therapy is particularly effective as it tackles problems from two sides – the actual behaviour of the couple and the psychological implications and sources of the problem.

Problems in achieving an erection

If you have problems in achieving an erection, your first port of call is to see your GP. Some forms of erection loss can occur because of illness or disease – diabetes or multiple sclerosis, for example. Some kinds of drugs can also adversely affect erectile response – for instance, some treatments for stomach ulcers can result in temporary loss of erection. Physical causes of erection loss are often treatable or, at the very least, can explain the loss. This is often comforting for a couple, particularly if the woman had felt that it had to do with the relationship and had not responded to initiatives taken by the couple. However, erection loss *is* often linked to psychological issues that have not been resolved. Sometimes it is a mixture of mild physical problems and psychological difficulties and treating only one part of the problem may not resolve the issue. Working at the concern from both a medical and psychological perspective can be extremely effective; this may involve the services of both a GP or medical specialist and a qualified psychosexual therapist.

Erection loss that is caused by a strong psychological component can often be affected by 'performance anxiety'. This kind of anxiety often goes through the following phases:

1. During sex, the man loses his erection either totally or partially. Sometimes the erection loss occurs before penetration actually happens or after the man has penetrated the woman. This may appear to happen out of the blue or may have happened occasionally before. The man is understandably concerned and may or may not talk to his partner about the event.
2. Between acts of love-making, the man begins to worry. Sometimes this worrying is conscious and sometimes it occurs at a subconscious level. He worries that the same thing will happen again and may search for ways to stop the event.
3. When the couple begin to make love the next time, the man is acutely aware of his anxiety. He watches (sometimes called 'spectatoring' by therapists) for the slightest sign that he is about to

lose his erection again. This anxiety prevents him from feeling aroused and probably releases chemicals in the brain that actually act against an erection occurring.

4. If he then loses his erection, the circle of anxiety intensifies. The next time he attempts sex, the anxiety may be so intense that the erection fails more quickly or never happens at all.

5. The man may avoid any sexual encounters. The couple may argue or the woman may convince herself that the problem is her fault – perhaps that her sexual technique is wrong – or that he has a mistress and has lost interest in her. These secret or overt concerns cause the couple to become distanced and sex may become a taboo subject.

Erection difficulties need the attention of both partners because they are usually connected to the relationship in some way. For example, the woman may be sympathetic to the man who loses his erection but could equally as well be accusing or mocking. The most important thing for the couple is that the man's anxiety about the erection is diminished rather than inflated. This can be accomplished by reading the section above on relaxing, which can counteract anxiety. The couple may also find it helpful to agree not to attempt to make love for a week or two. It is important to fix a time limit on this agreement or you may find that the 'sex ban' goes on too long and adds to anxiety rather than preventing it. During this time you should plan some sessions of touching and caressing in an intimate way. Use massage and sensuous exploration of each other's bodies, but do not attempt intercourse. The woman should stimulate the man by caressing and rubbing his penis. While this is happening, the man should relax and allow the sensual sensations to wash over him. This alone may cause the man's erection to return. Once the man feels less worried that his erection will fail, the couple can return to having intercourse. If the erection is still a problem, making an appointment to see a psychosexual therapist could be a valuable first step towards unravelling the problem.

Loss of erection can mask a loss of desire, for obvious reasons. A busy working life where you are expected to deliver to tight deadlines can cause tiredness and emotional exhaustion, leading to a loss of interest in sex. If you suffer from erectile difficulties it is important to look at the whole of your life rather than just what happens in the bedroom. Many men see their masculinity as wrapped up in how they perform at work, at home, in competition with friends and in bed. A failure in one area – such as a redundancy – can affect behaviour in other areas, including love-making. Loss of erection is rarely just a problem caused by something that is done or not done in sex. Understanding the causes of tension elsewhere in your life can help you to take action and restore your sexual feelings long before the erectile difficulty becomes entrenched.

Painful sex

While men *can* suffer from sex that hurts, the problem is much more likely to happen in women. The official name for this condition is 'dyspareunia'. It means that intercourse is painful and occasionally that stimulation of the labia and clitoris is also painful. Dyspareunia can be caused by some medical conditions – thrush, for instance, a condition that causes itching and discomfort in the vagina and on the outer vaginal lips and resembles nappy rash in a baby. Any attempt by a woman to make love if she has thrush can cause a burning sensation and pain. This is why seeing a GP is important so that this kind of medical problem can be ruled out before the couple attempt to try to sort the problem out for themselves.

Once medical causes have been eliminated, it may emerge that the painful sex is caused by psychological difficulties or by sexual technique that has gone astray. The most common cause of dyspareunia is time. By this I mean that lack of time is the greatest culprit in contributing to painful sex. Here is how dyspareunia can be made much worse:

1. The couple are already tired when they fall into bed. They would like to make love but feel exhausted by work and childcare. They decide to make love but attempt penetration very quickly. The woman is not properly aroused and as the man enters her she

feels a pinching, sometimes pulling, kind of pain. In response to the pain, her muscles clench and the pain feels worse because of the tension.

2. Next time the couple attempt to make love, the woman clenches her muscles around the vagina in anticipation of the pain. This makes it much more difficult for her partner to penetrate her and she receives the message that intercourse is painful.

3. If this goes on for a few months, the dyspareunia can prevent intercourse happening at all. If the man cannot penetrate the woman, this is called vaginismus; the woman experiences a spasm at the entrance to the vagina which stops anything entering the vagina, including fingers as well as a penis.

Dyspareunia is common after childbirth and gynaecological operations, but is mainly caused by a lack of sexual arousal. In order for intercourse to be pain-free for a woman she needs to be aroused by foreplay. This should last long enough for her to have sufficient lubrication and for the vagina to expand to accommodate a penis. This will take about twenty to thirty minutes in most women, although each woman is unique in how quickly she responds to arousal. One way to ensure that the woman enjoys a long enough arousal time is to agree a 'love pact' with a partner. In the pact, the couple decides they will have at least thirty minutes (or whatever seems appropriate) of mutual arousal before proceeding to intercourse. If the woman has had long-term problems with painful sex, the man should proceed by only allowing the tip of the penis into the vagina, gradually allowing more of the penis to enter as the woman becomes more confident. Extra lubrication can also be helpful. The best-known lubricant is probably KY Jelly (available at chemists and supermarkets), but there are others – Senselle by Durex is also good and simulates a woman's natural lubricant. Using a lubricant during sex play can also help the woman to feel more confident and less anxious about intercourse.

The best way to defeat dyspareunia is to prevent the tiredness that leads to fast and dissatisfying sex in the first place. Cutting work hours, dividing housework and daily chores, sharing childcare and taking an early night occasionally can all prevent the lack of arousal that leads to painful sex. I have worked with some women in psychosexual therapy who achieved orgasm for the first time after slowing down their sex and taking time to become properly aroused. There can be added benefits to approaching sex as if it were a stroll in the country rather than a race on a motorway! Of course, occasional fast and passionate sex can be exciting and good, but this should be a mutual decision rather than an act forced upon you because you are too tired to do anything else.

Competitive sex

No, this is not a new Olympic event alongside competitive swimming! By this I mean the feeling that the career couple may experience of having to be right up to date on every new sexual technique. Some couples worry that if they have not tried every new trick described in *Cosmopolitan* or *FHM* they are falling behind their friends who, they imagine, are swinging from lampshades every night. In the New Millennium we are bombarded by ideas about sex in a way that would have astounded our grandparents. The truth is that there are only so many ways to make love and most of what we read and hear about are variations on a theme. All of them have been thought of before and can be read about in old Asian chronicles as well as seen depicted on historic Asian temples, not to mention ancient Chinese 'pillow books' (sex guides). You are unique and have a sex life that is just yours. You do not have to compete or follow sexual trends, any more than you have to buy an orange and purple inflatable armchair for your lounge because your Sunday newspaper supplement says you should. Celebrate your uniqueness and originality by enjoying the sex you have. So what if you do not like some of the things that are currently in vogue? Be yourselves and you will enjoy what you do.

Unbalanced sexual desire

This is a common difficulty and is certainly experienced by career couples because of what you have already read about desire and its link to stress and tiredness. When one of you wants to make love and the other does not, it can often be connected to the stress that the resistant partner is under at the time. If the partner who wants sex does not understand this it can cause problems for both partners that may result in arguments. Explaining to your partner why you feel unable to make love is important. Saying something like 'I just don't want to' in reply to a question about why you do not want sex is not an explanation. You might also be able to offer a promise for the future. For instance, you might say 'I promise to make love next Wednesday when I have finished the project I am involved in.' If you do this, you must keep your promise or your partner may lose faith in you.

Problems with an imbalance in sexual desire can also be caused by a kind of power game. You may, consciously or unconsciously, want to control your partner, and use sex as a weapon to make them do as you want. For instance, you might deny sex if your partner works unsociable hours or grant sexual favours if they appear to be willing to put their office papers away for the weekend. To a certain degree this is inevitable in relationships. But to use sex in this cynical way can cause your relationship to feel like a business rather than a true relationship.

Re-balance your relationship by asking yourself why you are saying no to sex. If you are worn out or just too pushed for time, say so and try to arrange a more relaxed time later. If you are scoring points for some private game, try to analyse why you are doing this. It is better to talk about your feelings than spend your time trying to get some kind of revenge or 'one-upmanship' over your partner. A chronic imbalance in your sex life may suggest that things are OK once you start to make love, but one of you has trouble in initiating sex. You can manage this by agreeing to take turns in asking for sex and also agreeing a time period in which this has to happen. For instance, you may usually make love once a week, so agree that one partner asks one week while the other partner asks the following week. This can help you to become used to sharing the initiating, rather than one partner seeming always to be the pursuer and the other always the pursued.

Chapter review

This chapter has been concerned with career couples and their sexual relationships. The chapter began with information about common reasons for sexual problems and moved on to look at the sexual myths that couples often encounter. Practical ideas were given about improving sex, including useful ideas on relaxation, communicating successfully and improving body confidence. The chapter closed with practical help for sexual problems, outlining those most commonly encountered by busy working couples.

6

Problem busting –
facing common concerns
of career couples

All couples encounter difficulties. Some can be minor, others tougher to overcome. But the career couple face some particular issues that require special attention. Most of the problems that they encounter are linked to one particular issue – time. Time is the commodity that all career couples feel is in short supply. Some researchers into work and family life argue that the busy career couple actually work hard to buy time. For instance, they may buy expensive ready-prepared meals to cut down time spent in the kitchen so that they can work longer, thus creating a cycle of time deprivation. It might be logical to suggest that career couples should work less or take jobs that are less demanding, though perhaps less well paid, in order to have the time to do the things they want. For most career couples this is not usually an option, although 'downshifting' to a less stressful work situation has become more popular in recent years. Usually, career couples aspire to a certain lifestyle and believe that the hard work they undertake is worth any lack of private time in order to have the lifestyle they choose. Added to this is the understandable sense of self-esteem and personal creativity that succeeding in a chosen career can bestow. This chapter looks at particular issues that face career couples and offers some practical solutions, so that time spent together is less stressful and allows the couple to enjoy their relationship. The chapter will also include specific advice on issues that career couples may hope they never have to face, such as office affairs and sexual harassment at work, both of which can have a damaging effect on couples.

Managing family life when you both work

As discussed earlier in this book, the establishment of a routine is a great help when managing life as a career couple. It is even more important when you have children, because inconsistency in bringing up children is damaging and disables their ability to trust others in later life. You may also feel that living in a chaotic environment is difficult, preventing you from doing simple things as well as working at your best. A constant feeling of being 'at sea' will also lead to arguments and unhappiness because you may never feel properly in touch with yourself, your partner and others in the family. It is perfectly *possible* to live in a mess, never sure of where you left your diary or the last phone bill, but this can also be extremely stressful when you live with other people who depend upon you to help them cope with their own lives. The repeated search for car keys or a school lunch box can be funny on the first day it happens but soon wears thin on the twenty-first day. In this situation it is easy for couples to hurl recriminations at their partner, and this can eventually lead to a cooling of feelings between them. Here are some practical suggestions for creating an order that allows for the smooth running of family life as well as giving time for shared leisure.

Household chores

For many career couples, this is the crunch point in a relationship. For most people, domestic chores are boring, usually because they come round again and again, leading to a sense of futility. There are, of course, people who enjoy a particular task, such as ironing, because they find the mundane relaxing and a break from an otherwise more demanding work-life. You may not actively choose to do housework, but arguments about housework are one of the top issues for couples. Interestingly, a survey by Relate, the couple counselling charity, found that a partner doing too little housework was more likely to cause an argument for couples whose income was above £20,000 per annum than for those in lower income brackets. This may suggest that lack of time and pressure of work for those working longer hours and carrying more responsibility cause pressures to develop at home over who does what and when. Unfortunately, statistics demonstrate that men do less housework than women, even when both partners work. So to prevent repeated rows over household chores, try the following exercise:

Start by making an extensive list of all the chores that have to be done each week. Leave childcare arrangements out of this list, as we will deal with these later. Now categorise them in a grid, like this:

Chore	Prefer	Do not mind	Dislike
Cleaning bathroom			
Washing car			
Hoovering upstairs and downstairs			
Washing up/loading dishwasher			
Washing clothes/taking clothes to dry cleaners			

Chore	Prefer	Do not mind	Dislike
Dusting			
Weeding the garden			

And so on – fill in your own list of tasks that need to be tackled in the course of a week. Now, individually, tick each task in the appropriate column. If you enjoy gardening, tick the *prefer* column. If you are indifferent to washing up, tick the *do not mind* column and if you really hate washing the car, tick the *dislike* column. Do this for each item on your list.

Now compare your lists. You are likely to find that each of you has picked a few items that you actively prefer to do, chosen a majority of tasks you are indifferent about and listed a few that you dislike. Correlate your lists so that you can easily see which tasks can immediately be given to each partner and agree that you will undertake the *prefer* tasks you have listed. If you have doubled up in this list, agree to take turns on this chore, perhaps alternating days, weeks or months, depending on the actual nature of the task. Look at your *do not mind* lists and make a straightforward division of labour, unless you decide to swap the items on this list in a regular way. Now tackle the *dislike* list. With luck, some of the items on your list will appear in other columns on your partner's. You may hate ironing but find your partner prefers it, for example. If you have lots of shared *dislike* items, agree to take turns at doing them. Be clear about your joint expectations and review your lists every couple of months because your tasks may change over a period of time.

The alternative to drawing up a list of this kind is actually to employ someone to help out with the cleaning, or with just one domestic task you both hate. For instance, ironing services are springing up around the country that will do your ironing for you and deliver it to your door when finished. If you can afford to do this, it can really lift the pressure of domestic work. It may be worth doing this at an especially pressured time for the two of you – perhaps when you need to work away from your home or after an illness, for example. If you decide to find a house cleaner, you should follow these simple rules to ensure your own security and that you get the cleaner you want. These suggestions are also true for other services you may decide to employ, such as gardening.

- Seek a cleaner through a reputable agency. Ask the agency representative to meet you at your home and give a clear description of what you want a cleaner to undertake, as well as specifying the number of hours you require each week or day. Alternatively, ask your friends to recommend a cleaner they have used and feel confident about. Remember that you will now be an employer and must be responsible for making payments regularly, as well as checking standards of work.
- Check any references you receive by phoning the person who gave the reference. You are inviting a stranger into your home so it is important that you are free from the worry of leaving your personal property in their care.
- Once you have found a cleaner, make sure you are both clear about hours of work and hourly fee. Remember that you must now pay the minimum wage of £3.60 per hour. Fix the most appropriate day(s) you would like the cleaner to come. Check whether he or she will bring their own cleaning materials or will use yours. Ask if the cost of the cleaning materials is included in his or her hourly rate, or will be a separate cost to you. Keep a written record of your agreements.
- Ask if they might occasionally be willing to take on extra tasks such as cleaning the oven for an extra payment.
- Negotiate about holiday payments. Your cleaner may expect a retainer or this could be handled by the agency, if you use one.

Whether you choose a cleaner, gardener, car valet service or deal with chores yourself, it is worth investing some time in sorting out what you will do about everyday tasks. Once you have a routine working well, you may not notice how the tasks are performed because they have become an established part of your life. Far from turning you into a boring couple who wash the car every Sunday morning, you can free up valuable time for things you would much rather do – like making love or water-skiing! You may also find that once you have maintained a routine for a while, you can make alterations that do not require weeks of negotiations and stand-offs about whose turn it is to clean the toilet. Swapping tasks occasionally and agreements to undertake together a regular but occasional job such as cutting a hedge or trimming garden shrubs can improve your communication and relieve the boredom of finding that you are always left with the shopping or grass mowing.

Working through childcare

Earlier in the book there is extensive help in choosing childcare for your family. This section is about how you manage the mechanics of being parents when you both work. When the baby is small it is important to begin talking about how you will manage childcare when you are both back at work. Expectations that this is solely the mother's area of care are still rife, so that the female partner often feels that she has to take full responsibility for not only arranging childcare but also picking up and dropping off the child, or negotiating with the nanny or live-in help. While some women are perfectly happy to do this, many feel that they are expected to have full responsibility for this area on top of an already busy lifestyle. It is better if the male partner can share the responsibilities for coping with childcare, at the very least because the mother may be ill or unavailable at some time. More importantly, this also helps the father to feel fully involved with all the aspects of his child's life. A sense of belonging is vital for all the members of the family. In order to decide how you might handle decisions about future arrangements, you need to gaze into the crystal ball.

- First of all, try to reflect on your work arrangements as they stand. Be practical. Discuss how early you have to be in your workplace and what time you normally finish. Take into account shift work and overtime. Then work backwards from this time and calculate how long it might take you to get the baby ready and travel to the carer and then to work. This should give you both a start time for getting up and how long your trip is likely to be in the morning. Do the same for the evening. You may discover that it would be most efficient, for instance, if one of you drops the child off in the morning and the other picks the child up in the evening. If there is a problem, perhaps because of a difficulty in reaching your workplace in time, alert your line manager or personnel officer so that a solution can be found. For instance, you may be able to arrange flexi-time working for a few months.

- Next, talk through how you will handle the evenings, especially if you have a small child that needs undressing, bathing and settling. You may opt for a simple solution such as taking turns throughout the week. Alternatively, you could split the tasks so that whoever baths the child then cooks the evening meal while the other partner puts them to bed. You could swap roles the next night. This allows for greater variety and is a good model for the child, who sees that both parents can be nurturing. Discuss how you might manage this if one of you has to take on extra work or is away from home.

- As your child grows older he or she will begin to be able to do small tasks for themselves – dressing and eating without assistance. Encourage them in this so that they can be relatively independent and this will smooth the morning and evening routines. It can seem more time consuming at the start as you long to put their arms in the right armholes or do up their shoelaces, particularly if you are in a hurry. If you can be patient it will pay dividends in the future, because the child will be better able to take responsibility for itself as it grows up.

- Encourage a routine once the child starts school. For instance, set a 'getting up' time, making sure that their school clothes are ready to wear. Allow enough time for washing and eating breakfast as well as the time it takes to travel to school. If the child is capable, allow them to make their own lunch box, in the morning or the night before. Each child is unique, but praise and assistance will help them to feel that they can get themselves as ready as possible.

- Make sure that you maintain a good relationship with the school

147

so that you can deal with any problems that the child may encounter. Again, check out with your manager or personnel officer what company policy is concerning your attendance at school plays and parent/teacher meetings.

Ensuring that you have a sensible routine and understand what you expect from one another with your family commitments is important to your relationship. It may not seem obvious at the outset, but you will feel closer to one another if you are not constantly wrangling, day after day, over the children and what they need. Routines of this kind are also protective because they can act as scaffolding if you hit a difficulty.

Case Study

Sally and Nigel had been married for five years when they had their first child, David. From the start of their relationship they had divided their household tasks equally and agreed strategies for coping when Sally was away from home, which happened often as she acted as a representative for her company all over Europe. When David was born, Sally's plan was to return to work once she had taken her full maternity leave. They spent several evenings working out how they would manage David's care. They were fortunate in that Nigel's mother lived very close to them and she agreed to look after David while Nigel and Sally worked. They soon had a morning and evening routine well under way and all went well until David was just over a year old. Sally suddenly became very ill and was diagnosed as suffering from a lung disease. She was hospitalised for a few weeks and then convalesced at home. Nigel coped well with caring for David because he and Sally had shared everything and he knew as much about looking after David as Sally or his mother. With extra help from Nigel's mother, their shared routine saved the day because it also allowed Sally and Nigel to spend time together in the evenings as Sally gradually got better. Their relationship survived a stressful and worrying time because they had set up tried and tested ways of coping with their life. David also gained because he had the benefit of being cared for in a consistent way that allowed him to feel secure and settled. Despite the real concern for Sally's health, Nigel and Sally felt closer after her illness because they had worked together as a team and found that their planning had paid off.

When you work together

Couples who work together are much more common nowadays. This may be the result of greater equality for women or simply a greater recognition of women's contribution to businesses that have always required team work, such as pubs, shops and service industries. Whatever the case, working with your partner requires some special understanding that may not immediately be apparent when you first start out together. Many couples find that they set out full of hope that their business will work well, only to discover that, although the business may succeed, their relationship begins to falter. This may be partly due to differences between intimate and business relationships, but also to the number of assumptions made by partners who work together. In most businesses you have to work according to a contractual arrangement that spells out what is expected of you. You will probably also have to present any project you suggest for peer analysis and then modify the result according to your colleague's suggestions. In a relationship where you work together, you may take all this as read and jump straight into action, believing that your partner will automatically understand and co-operate. Here are some suggestions to help you sustain your intimate relationship when working together.

- Never assume your partner knows about or agrees with your schemes and strategies for the business. Discuss what is happening in mini 'board' meetings and do all the things you would normally do – prepare an agenda and minute what you discuss and any outcomes. Draw up contracts for each of you and ask a solicitor to check out what you have agreed. At the same time, ask the solicitor to explain any relevant company law, especially who is liable for what if the business fails. It is well worth the expense of doing this so that you set out on a firm footing.

- If you engage staff, do it together. Go through the correct selection and interview processes so that you both feel satisfied that you have chosen the best person for the job and agreed upon it. You may be tempted to give jobs to family members or friends, but think hard about how this could affect you or the business if problems develop later.

- Avoid blurring the lines between work and home. This may be difficult if you work from home, but try to create a watershed between work and home life. Agree not to discuss work over the dinner table and spend time at the end of your working day doing something that is totally unrelated to work – walking the dog or watching your favourite TV soap can help you switch off. If you cannot avoid discussing work outside normal working hours, agree a time limit so that you know the conversation cannot drag on until bedtime.

- If you feel that your partner is not pulling their weight, you must say so. Do not take more and more upon yourself because you fear that the business will fold if you do not take over. Try to discover the root of the problem and take action to solve it. For instance, Vic felt angry because he was doing more and more in the shop that he and his wife Rita ran together. Rita found it hard to carry out her usual tasks because she had learnt that their son was having an affair and planned to leave his marriage. Her worry over this matter caused her to become depressed and uninterested in work. When she plucked up courage to tell Vic, she found that he was relieved that there was a reason for her lack of enthusiasm. There was little they could actively do to solve their son's behaviour, but they shared their feelings about the problem and this helped Vic and Rita to cope more effectively with work.

- Be completely open about money and any financial issues that your shared business may face. Decide how much you should receive in salary and monitor the financial side of the business as a team. It could help to draw up contracts relating to the two of you and get these checked over by an expert in employment law. Avoid leaving it to just one partner, because you may not realise if there are mistakes or neglect of some kind. Do not set yourself up as the 'foreman', checking up on your partner's work. Instead, tackle the business records together. Ensure that you have a good relationship with your bank or building society so that any problems are dealt with quickly and efficiently. *Never* leave money problems to fester in the hope that they will 'just go away'. You could find your home at risk if you default on payments. This kind of trauma can break a relationship very quickly, so speedy action could save a lot more than your shared business.

- Take regular breaks and holidays. Some couples who work in shared businesses live in a 'promise' syndrome: 'We've promised ourselves a holiday when this order is out/we can get the staff/built up the customers' etc. Taking breaks from work is not a luxury but an essential. Weekends and a week or two away from the business are vital. If you cannot afford a holiday away, make sure you have time that is purely for the two of you or the family. Hire a video, make home-made popcorn and enjoy a film together or visit friends you have lost contact with – in fact, do anything that allows you to switch off work and feel connected to your roots with one another again.

Many couples make a success of working together, finding that the pleasure of sharing a business or new venture helps to cement their partnership. For others it can be stressful and difficult, but following the ideas listed above can make a real difference to your experience.

Working from home

One of the biggest revolutions that individuals and couples are experiencing is a silent one. People are beginning to work from home. This is happening because of advances in communication technology. It is possible to sit at a PC screen at home and contact people on the other side of the world through e-mail, fax machines, screen/video phones and a host of other innovations. For people (like me!) who communicate and work through the written word, this has brought about a new way of living and working. The back pages of many Sunday supplements now carry adverts for 'home office' furniture and the BBC has recently carried out a pilot study into resourcing journalists in their homes. This way of working carries many benefits – no long train or car journeys, adaptability in working hours and the chance to concentrate and avoid interruptions from work colleagues. It can also carry some problems. You may feel cut off from colleagues or torn between family and work, especially if your child demands your attention when you should be working, and there is the potential for work to 'bleed' into family life. As far as relationships are concerned, this is an issue that needs talking through and guidelines need to be drawn up before you make a final decision to relocate to a home base. The guidelines below can help you talk about how you should approach this modern style of working:

- Ensure you have a private space in which to work. Never set up a laptop on a table in the main family room because you will soon be distracted and irritated that you are unable to work because of interruptions. It is also not fair for your family to have to adapt to your working time when they may want to eat a meal or simply talk to one another. Try using a bedroom or boxroom as a small study. Take into account that you will need books and files as well as you and your PC.
- Stick to working times as far as possible. For instance, you may decide you need to work six hours a day to ensure you get all your work done. Decide that you will start work at 9.30 a.m., have a lunch break and finish work at 4.30 p.m. Occasionally you may need to give a day to something else – a swimming lesson with a child, for instance. In these circumstances you may need to work a couple of hours in the evening. Whatever you decide will be the normal rhythm of your day, talk it through with your partner. Spend each Sunday evening synchronising your diaries so that you have a good idea of what you are both doing in the week ahead.
- One of the key attributes of working from home is flexibility. You may feel free to cook a meal, fetch the children from school or do some shopping because you can make up an hour later. But this

flexibility is also a problem. You have the chance to work as you choose but this can soon spiral into a situation where you are constantly trying to juggle a lifestyle that feels out of control. Your family may also regard you as 'at home' and therefore available to supply lifts or clean the toilet when you should be working on a project for your employer. Creating a structure and being clear about your availability can prevent the worst of this situation. Small children are less likely to grasp this concept than older children, so you may need to help them understand your status in the house. There will be particular times when you need privacy and a 'do not disturb' notice on the door can be helpful to ensure this. Even toddlers can be helped to understand that the sign means they should not come in. You may have to work at this, but eventually your family will become accustomed to your occasional seclusion.

- If your partner is also at home – perhaps caring for children or also working from home – you can seize the right moment to make love, which is an often undisclosed reward of home working! With children at school, and a lunch break in your own kitchen instead of the company canteen, you can enjoy a lusty lunch and still carry on working in the afternoon!

- Take proper breaks. As with working with a partner, you need to take meal breaks and time off in the same way as if you worked in an office (although far too many people still eat a sandwich at their desk rather than get away from their office environment). If you work from home, leaving the house for half an hour at some point during the day can be very helpful. Take a walk or stroll round your garden to help you feel refreshed during your working day. Walk to the post office rather than drive – any activity that stretches your muscles and provides fresh air.

- Be organised. Buy a second-hand filing cabinet and keep papers and files locked away. This will prevent you losing papers around the house and ensure that work is kept firmly in its place instead of infiltrating every other area of your life. This can also help your partner to know that there is a clear delineation between him or her and your work. Your partner needs your personal attention and it is hard to give or receive this when you feel that your home is not a home but a workplace.

- Avoid the temptation to take phone calls or read e-mails during couple or family time. Make use of an answerphone and save e-mails until your designated work time. Of course, there will be times when you have to answer an urgent call, but make sure that this does not slide into answering every call because it *might* be urgent. Monitor the answerphone, only picking up the call if it really does require an immediate answer.

Working from home does have significant benefits for a couple. You can see each other easily and interact more naturally because you are not out of the house for long periods. You may be able to be flexible in arranging work that takes account of family concerns and enjoy spending time with your family that is not curtailed by travelling to and from work. But it does require discipline and commitment from you and your family so that you can work properly. Using the guidelines above can really help you to make a success of your home working.

Holidays – pleasures or pains?

Most couples look forward to holiday times and this is certainly true when both partners in a relationship work. Holidays can help you to renew your relationship and give time to talking and having fun which is often in short supply during the working week. But lots of couples find holidays a mixed blessing. They find that they argue or feel distant from their partner during the holiday rather than feel closer. Expectations and hopes about the holiday can be spoilt by seemingly trivial problems that put a damper on your holiday mood. Here is how to have a holiday that sets you up to return to working life but also improves your closeness to your partner.

- **Prepare well**
  Pick a holiday that is within your means and that you will both enjoy. You may be tempted to buy an expensive holiday, but if you have to work hours of overtime to pay for it the benefit of the holiday will soon disappear. Find a holiday you feel comfortable with and you will enjoy it much more because you will not be constantly worrying that you have overspent. When you choose a holiday, make sure that you all have a shared expectation of what you want. If you want to lie by the hotel pool while your partner expects the two of you to go hill walking, you have the recipe for a miserable time. Negotiate over any differences – perhaps by agreeing to alternate activities each day, or by choosing a dual-site holiday.

- **Share the packing and other arrangements**
  If one of you has to shoulder the lion's share of getting ready to go away, you may find that you arrive with a bag full of resentment alongside your suitcases. This will set up arguments and coldness for the early days of your trip. If it really is hard to share the packing, make sure that you both have tasks that will help the holiday to start well. For instance, Ben had to work long hours in the run up to his holiday with Greta. They agreed that Greta would take care of the packing but Ben would arrange holiday money and organise tickets because he worked close to the town centre.

Have long enough away to be able to relax

Short breaks can be good if you take them regularly – perhaps instead of a long holiday – but many couples describe the phenomenon of taking a few days to wind down and then a few days to wind up to returning to work. If this is true for you, two weeks in a less expensive resort may be better than a week in a costly centre. Alternatively, book a few more days of leave than you are actually away so that you can feel ready to leave or return to work. If you work together in a shared business, ensure that you have booked staff to cover for you and feel confident that they can cope with the business while you are away. Greg and Debbie were joint landlords in their own pub and looked forward to their holidays a great deal because they worked long, often anti-social, hours. They usually booked the same staff to work in the pub while they were away because they felt they could trust their business to them. Using trusted staff, or training staff to manage the business during your absence, can help you to feel able to let go of work while you are away.

- *Once you are on holiday, talk about what you want to happen*
  If there are special excursions you want to try or restaurants you want to eat at, make sure you have discussed this with your partner. As in other areas of your relationship, unsupported assumptions that your partner will want what you want can ruin a longed-for holiday. Try to alternate days of activity with days of rest. It is important to have time simply to empty your mind of stress and although you may also feel relaxed touring local ruins or wind-surfing, you need the opportunity to let go of schedules and activity as well. Exercise can be good for improving your self-esteem, so dancing at the local club or beach volleyball may also help you to relax. However much you enjoy your work, getting away from the routine and demands of work is crucial if you want to go on enjoying it.

Allow for some space between you

You might find it helpful to spend a little time apart on holiday. Henry and Annie always went to the same Portuguese resort for their yearly holiday because they loved the atmosphere and had grown to know the locals. They had agreed years before that they would allow each other some freedom to be alone if they wished. Henry enjoyed walking the coastline near to their resort while Annie liked visiting the local market. They usually agreed on two days each week to spend apart on these individual pleasures and found that they enjoyed sharing what they had done at the end of the day. You may not need a whole day like Henry and Annie, but you might appreciate an hour or two to do something that only you would like.

Discuss childcare

If you intend to holiday with your family, it is important to think about how you will handle childcare. Do not expect one partner to do all the caring, because this will probably not be a holiday for them and the children will feel short-changed. This is particularly true if one partner (often the mother) undertakes most of the care. In these circumstances, your children may be looking forward to spending playtime with the other partner and could feel that they have lost the opportunity to be with the partner they see least. It is also possible that the partner who cares most for the children can privately decide that he or she intends to have a holiday from the routines of childcare and will expect the other partner to look after them for the whole holiday. Talk about the practicalities of managing childcare. For example, you might decide to take a holiday where there is some childcare provision laid on or pick a resort where there is plenty for children to do all day. Discuss how you will share care of your children. You might decide to divide each day into sections and agree that you will care for the children in different sections, or simply decide that you will both play with and look after your children together rather than leave it to one partner alone. Whatever you decide, the crucial thing is that you agree and talk through what should happen rather than hope it will work out on the day. You should also make sure that you have adequate insurance and access to medical care when travelling with children (although this is also important to you as adults) so that you can feel relatively safe if an accident occurs.

- ### *Be careful about drinking and eating too much*

  It is natural to want to dispense with your normal restraints on holiday and to some extent there is not much harm in eating foods you would normally avoid at home – particularly those high in calories – or drinking a little more. Relationship problems can come along when the holiday turns into mornings spent nursing a hangover or feeling sick due to over-indulgence the night before. Boozy nights can not only ruin your partnership but also your sex life. Alcohol can have a depressant effect on libido and can cause physical difficulties with arousal for both men and women. Moderate your drinking and eating and the holiday can fulfil all your expectations instead of becoming an argument zone.

- *Talk about your holiday sex life*
  You may both be expecting to make love more and many couples do find that the relaxation on holiday helps sex to be more passionate. Alternatively, you may find that you need to get to know each other and feel intimate again. This can be especially true if you have seen little of each other because you have been working hard in the months before the holiday. If this is true for you, start by increasing touching and affection, building up to love-making after a couple of days, rather than making love straight away. All couples pass through this dance of distance versus closeness during their relationship and it can help to know that you are capable of repairing a sense of distance with warmth and understanding. Learning this on holiday can stand you in good stead once you are back home.

Most couples would agree that holidays and breaks are essential to maintain sanity whilst holding down a job. This is not to suggest that all work is so boring or exhausting that you only work for your holidays. Lots of people enjoy their working life and carry out jobs that are creative and exciting. But in order to go on enjoying your job it is important to allow time for your mind and body to recuperate so that you are fresh for work and home life after the holiday. The old saying 'All work and no play makes Jack a dull boy' is still true. Some couples feel that short breaks taken at regular times throughout the year are preferable, whereas others like to save up their holiday time in order to have a longer break. You must decide what options are right for you and your family. Whatever you decide, enjoying a holiday together can strengthen your relationship and help you to feel secure in your partnership.

The career couple and infidelity

Most couples report that an affair is the most dreaded problem they are likely to encounter. Statistics suggest that more men than women have affairs and that more professional working men have affairs than any other group. This may be because, until recently, more men than women have been in paid work and therefore had opportunities to meet other people outside their committed relationship. All this may be set to change as women take up careers and jobs previously only thought suitable for men. The office affair is still well known and can cause a relationship to fail. Affairs, however, are not the cause of relationship failure. They are symptoms of already existing problems of which the couple may be conscious or unconscious.

Case Study

Tom and Eva had been married for four years when Tom admitted an affair. He had met a woman, Carol, at a conference and slept with her. He told Eva he had met Carol a few times since the conference but felt little for her, describing the relationship as just a 'sexual thing'. Eva, however, saw things very differently. She felt devastated and rejected by Tom's behaviour. She took a lot of the blame for the affair on her own shoulders, telling herself it was due to her tiredness and loss of interest in sex during the previous six months. Eva worked in PR and had just launched a big campaign that had left her feeling drained and distant from Tom because she had been away from home a great deal. Tom's response was to expect Eva to forget the whole thing and accept him as he had always been. Eva could not do this. She felt that her self-esteem had been flattened and she lost her trust in Tom. Tom and Eva had an extremely difficult year following the affair and lived apart for a few months, but came to realise that Tom's affair had been caused by long-standing problems in the relationship. Neither had felt close to the other before the affair. Eva described this phase as living 'parallel lives' – they had shared a home but rarely talked about their life or plans for the future. The affair acted as a diagnosis of the problems they had been experiencing and ultimately helped them to see that the affair was not the problem but that their marriage needed immediate attention.

People have affairs for many reasons. Sometimes they want to escape a relationship which they know in their heart is already over and so they set up a new partnership. Others have an affair in an (often unconscious) attempt to alert their partner to the perilous state of the relationship. Some affairs serve to create an emotional distance between the person having the affair and their committed partner – perhaps because they find emotional intimacy too hard to cope with. Often they are the outcome of a desire to be found attractive, especially if a committed partner appears not to notice their partner in a meaningful way.

Whatever the deeper cause, affairs can be triggered by life events. Bereavement, children leaving home, the birth of a child, job changes, age-related events such as reaching a certain age of significance to the person and recovery from illness can all provoke affairs. It is wise to use the skills described earlier in this book to cultivate the ability to communicate successfully, as this can help to head off an affair. Maintaining a relationship where you can see each other regularly and relax together is important. Affairs often blossom when the person having the affair can justify it to themselves, believing that their partner will not know or care about it. Unfortunately, secret affairs can have just as harmful an effect on a relationship because they alter the way in which the person having the affair behaves towards their partner. This change is often subtle but can, over time, cause the relationship to feel 'less real'. Deception is no ground on which to build a partnership, particularly if you are both working hard and need to trust your partner to carry out promises and act as part of a team with you.

Preventing an affair

- Talk to one another about your feelings and hopes for the future in a consistent and regular way. Put time aside to be alone together and make a real effort to keep communication flowing between you, even if you argue or feel miserable with each other (*especially* at these times).

- Be tolerant and understanding of your partner during periods of change. Be alert to change and expect it to put some strain on you both. Talk about how you can support one another if you know the change is imminent, and be thoughtful if it is unexpected. For instance, Beryl's mother died suddenly of a heart attack. Beryl was knocked sideways by the death and found it hard to discuss with Colin, her husband of twenty years. Colin felt sidelined, and unable to reach Beryl. He started talking to a kind woman colleague at work and found himself on the brink of an affair just when Beryl needed him most. Colin realised he could endanger his marriage and drew back, resolving to try to reach Beryl by talking to her and being there for her when she needed him.

- Keep your own sense of self-esteem alive. If you work hard and feel that life is mostly work, eat and sleep, your sense of self-esteem may gradually fade away. Instead of seeing yourself as an interesting person who has plenty to share with your partner, you may begin to feel grey and boring. If you feel this way it can communicate itself to your partner who may feel that you also lack interest in the partnership. Maintain an interest in leisure pursuits or anything that you have enjoyed in the past. Simple things like playing chess or reading can be just as effective as dry slope skiing or deep sea diving! The most important thing is to do things that help you to feel good about yourself. This might include having regular haircuts, an aromatherapy session, or buying new shoes. Do whatever is within your means to do, but be careful of doing this kind of thing to please your partner. Take action because you want or need to, rather than because you feel you must look or behave a certain way to keep your partner. Self-esteem is just that – yours alone to determine. It is true that pleasing yourself can also please a partner so that the relationship gains, but try to think about your own goals and dreams as much as your partner's.

- Think about your satisfaction with your sex life. It is a common misconception that affairs are all about sexual desire. They are often much more complex and connected to more general difficulties in the relationship, not just the couple's sex life. But it is possible that a troubled sexual relationship may act as a catalyst for an individual to feel justified in seeking a sexual fling. Reread Chapter Five to help you overcome any sexual problems you may face. If this is an ongoing problem in your relationship, you could benefit from seeing a psychosexual therapist (see the Further help section at the back of the book for contacts).

- Be honest with one another about what is happening at work. You may think it is simpler to avoid telling your partner about the flirting that goes on in the office, or even the direct invitation to dinner, because you do not want to alarm them, but it is much better to be open. This is because if you lie or omit the truth it may gradually set up a psychological distance between work and home that becomes a barrier. Once this happens, you may feel it is OK to have an affair at work because of the emotional separateness of your work and home life. In other words, try to see your life in a holistic way, connected rather than separated by invisible walls.

Coping if an affair happens

If you find yourself trying to cope with an affair, you may experience lots of different emotions. Some people who have been through an affair describe it as feeling like a bereavement. This is a good description because in a sense the relationship you knew has died. Despite all your longing, the relationship you once had can never be the same again. You may be able to repair or rebuild your partnership and it may emerge stronger, but it will be different to the relationship you had before the affair. This may be a good thing, especially if the relationship that led to the affair was strained and under stress, but you will probably still feel sadness for the loss.

Here are some suggestions to help you cope with an affair.

Stage 1
In the early stages of discovery – from finding out to two or three months after the affair is revealed
During this period you are likely to feel numb and in shock. You may go through periods when you cannot believe the affair has really happened and deny it to yourself or your partner. This can be followed by times of intense emotion – anger, shame, depression or jealousy. You may verbally attack your partner or make snap decisions about the future of the partnership – such as demanding that your partner should leave.

Stage 2
In the mid-stage after discovery – from three months to eight or nine months after revelation of the affair.
During this time you may vacillate between feeling extremely angry and upset and long periods of sadness and self-blame. You may also find yourself wanting to ask lots of questions about the affair and the other person involved. You may decide to stay together or part during this time, but this decision will be influenced by the type of commitment you have to the relationship and whether you have children.

Stage 3
In the late stage after the discovery of the affair – from nine months to two years after the affair
If you decide to stay together, this is the period during which you will gradually remake your relationship. You will need to build up a sense of trust between you that is proven by actions as well as promises. You may decide to move house or jobs, especially if the other person in the affair lives nearby or works with the partner who had the affair. Your sex life may take this long to recover and you may have to work hard at restoring a sense of closeness. Intimacy is often the last part of a relationship to recover after an affair.

What to do during each stage

During Stage 1

- Be wary of making snap decisions about staying in or ending the relationship. Give yourselves time to allow the significance of the affair to sink in so that you feel able to take in what has happened to you.
- Ask questions if you need to, but be aware that the answers can make your grief feel worse for a while, even if you do eventually need to know the truth about what happened.
- Try to understand why the affair happened. It is natural to want to blame the person who had the affair and/or their lover, but this will not help you resolve any underlying concerns that led to the affair in the first place.
- Allow yourself to weep or yell if you need to. Try not to become physically aggressive as this will make things much worse whatever you decide to do in the long run.

During Stage 2

- Be aware of your changing feelings and accept them as natural at this stage. You may want to feel certain about the future and secure again, but your equilibrium has been severely disturbed and you may make a decision one day only to reverse it the next.
- Avoid taking vengeance on your partner's lover. You may want to hurt them in some way but you are extremely likely to regret this later. This is a natural response, partly because at an unconscious level you may want to exonerate your partner from blame, choosing to see the lover as a seducer or persuader. The truth is that it always takes two to create an affair. Blaming the lover will not help you to make sense of the causes of the affair and this is crucial if the relationship is to continue or you are to part with any understanding of what went wrong.
- If you want the relationship to continue, you must be brave and face the reasons why the affair occurred. Look back over the previous couple of years and search for changes or tricky issues you may not have handled well or been able to bring yourself to

face. Talk about these and decide how you want to handle things now. For instance, Jake realised that his habit of bringing copious amounts of paperwork home at weekends had contributed to Gemma seeking more of a social life without him and consequently beginning an affair. Jake agreed to stop working all weekend and he and Gemma set about resurrecting a relationship where they had more fun.

During Stage 3

- If you have stayed together, this is the stage where you will need to work hard at building trust. If you make promises to each other, you must be scrupulous in keeping them. Make an effort to share your feelings about particular concerns in your relationship. This will not be easy, but if you can break through what is sometimes a 'pain barrier' your relationship will be the stronger.

- Talk about sex. Again, be honest about how the affair has made you feel. You may feel guilty, or not want to have sex because of the betrayal, but this can be overcome if you gradually begin to feel you can trust your partner. It can be helpful to put off intercourse until you are both more confident. Instead, give a massage or just cuddle. It is natural for the unhappy memories of the affair to disturb your sex life. You may want to prove that you are as good a lover as the person your partner had the affair with by having sex with your unfaithful partner, or you may feel physically repulsed by sex. Either of these responses is normal, but you need to give yourself time to feel happy about love-making again.

- Draw up a new contract for your relationship. This should consist of the things you expect to happen now that you are starting again or stipulate what will happen if you betray or are betrayed again. Avoid a list of rules to 'control' the erring partner. Instead, think about what you want now and add in expectations for both of you. If you have identified areas from the past that may have contributed to the affair tackle these so that they can be dealt with in the future.

Managing social issues at work

Romantic relationships in the office

Many career couples meet through work, or at least a shared interest in similar work. While this is understandable, others do not always view the office romance with equanimity. Some companies actually forbid romantic relationships in the workplace, while others lack an overt policy and simply frown on them. Whatever the situation in your workplace, meeting and maintaining a relationship with an office colleague can be difficult to handle. If you are not expressly forbidden from going out together, the following rules can help you.

- *Do be honest with colleagues*
  Keeping your romance a secret, or lying about it, will only add to speculation in the office. Telling people will stop gossip and allow you to behave normally.

- *Do not hold hands by the photocopier or snog in the stationery cupboard*
  Not only is this unprofessional, but it will also diminish your status in the eyes of those you manage.

- *Do think about what conclusions your colleagues may draw from your relationship*
  For instance, if one of you is superior to the other they may feel that you will receive special favours, such as more time off when sick or a better chance on the promotional ladder. Consider transferring to another department or changing jobs to escape this problem.

Do not jump into an office romance
Christmas parties are not the time to decide that you must seduce the bloke from accounts you have always fancied or the girl you met at the company barbecue last summer. Each New Year sees people sheepishly returning to work after a drunken kiss and

cuddle they have come to regret. Watch what you drink – you will have to look at the object of your affections over the meeting-room table for the rest of the year. It is better to develop a friendship progressing to a closer relationship over a period of time.

- **Do avoid affairs of any kind, but especially those with people you work with**
Because you share an interest in the same kind of work you may make the mistake of believing that your colleague is closer to you than your partner. Once your affair faces the harsh light of reality – that is, life outside the office – you may realise that it is not what you want. Unfortunately, by then you could have thrown away a committed relationship.

Do face the music if the relationship ends
Tell people in the office it is over and consider if the end of your relationship means that you should make changes. For instance, Kerry asked for a transfer to another bank branch once her relationship with her banking colleague ended. She found it too painful to see him every day.

Office romances can be attractive because you have a ready source of shared interests and material to talk about. But this can be a down side if you spend all your time talking about work rather than having a complete break and discussing other topics. You should also bear in mind that others might not like the idea that you are talking about office issues – especially if one of you is superior to the other. You may need to talk this through with your personnel department if you intend to stay in the relationship. From a personal point of view, declare 'work-free zones' in the evenings and at weekends, promising not to discuss work and to do something different instead.

Some companies ask their staff to attend social events without their partners. The thinking behind this is usually concerned with fostering a sense of teamwork and camaraderie that will help the company to work well. But it can cause problems for the couple where one partner stays at home. They may be prey to jealousy or resentment, wondering what their partner is doing and whom they are with. Free-flowing drink or unusual surroundings can complicate this situation. For example, some companies hire leisure clubs or hotels that allow the employees to mix in a very different way to meeting in the factory canteen or office kitchen. You may find it useful to talk about some personal guidelines for behaviour when just one partner attends these events. Do not make demands, but suggest simple ideas that will help each partner to know where they stand. For example, Ellis promised his girlfriend that he would not drink more than three pints of beer at the office social event and would aim to be home by 1 a.m. This is not so much a question of lack of trust as a way of ensuring that each partner in a situation like this has a real sense of security.

Coping with sexual harassment

This may not seem an obvious topic for this book, but it can be a problem that you or your partner may face during your working life. As with other issues such as racism and ageism, sexual harassment is most often experienced in working life and can apply to men or women. It is not easy to define sexual harassment because it is a situation that only you can experience and know its effects. For some people it is a leering glance, for others offensive e-mails or pictures in the company mail and for still others the very unwanted touch from a colleague. People often do not speak out on harassment for fear of losing their job or looking foolish in front of others. Some people wait until they are sure that the accidental brush against them is no accident but a direct attempt to grope them. Whatever you experience, it is important to take action. Saying nothing when you feel uncomfortable may condemn others to enduring uninvited touching in the same way. It is never easy to be a whistle blower, but it can help others to come forward with similar complaints.

There is a well-known procedure to help you deal with harassment. Gain the emotional support of your partner as you tackle the problem and you will feel much more confident.

- *Keep a record of the harassment and any witnesses*
  You may wish to show your partner what you have written, but never suggest or allow your partner to take matters into their own hands. If they accuse or become aggressive towards the perpetrator of the harassment, this could count against you in any subsequent investigation.

- *Let the perpetrator know that you dislike their attentions*
  If necessary, write your complaint in a letter, keeping a copy for yourself.

- *Tell your line manager what is happening*
  If *they* are the perpetrator, tell a colleague you trust, your personnel manager or union representative. Ask them what action they intend to take and monitor this to ensure it actually happens.

- *If the harassment continues, seek legal help*
  Your solicitor may be able to advise you. Otherwise, the local Citizens Advice Bureau can also help you on what steps to take next. Act within three months of the last incident if you go to an industrial tribunal.

From an emotional viewpoint, if your partner suffers from sexual harassment they will need your support and care as they try to prevent it happening. They may even feel as if they have been sexually abused. He or she could pass through a phase of believing that they must have attracted the unwanted attentions, or feel afraid to go to work. It is crucial that you believe what your partner is saying and are willing to listen to them talk. Never suggest that it is 'a joke' or 'a mistake'. If your partner is upset by the incident(s) it has significance for him or her and should be taken seriously, however insignificant the harassment appears to you. Offer practical support, such as accompanying them to a law adviser, and give them plenty of encouragement and affection during the time they are dealing with the problem.

Career couples do encounter some particular problems, as this chapter demonstrates, but they can also benefit from a mutual understanding of the pleasures and strains of balancing home and work life. Here is Julian, a GP, explaining the benefits of being married to Fiona, who is a social worker.

Fiona and I understand, often without having to explain in detail, how work affects each of us. I know that I can tell Fiona I am tired and she will understand, just as I understand when she flops on the couch at the end of the day. We also put a lot of effort into our social life because we need the relaxation of switching off at weekends and on holiday. Although it has been tough at times, nobody else would understand like Fiona the ups and downs of working with people, and I think she feels the same as me. I love her for her empathy and I am sure our successful balance of home and work has given us a good relationship.

Chapter review

This chapter has covered common problems that a career couple may face and offered suggestions on how to cope with these. Typical problems are: managing the division of household chores, including how to appoint a cleaner if desired; coping with practical decisions about childcare; managing working together and working from home. Ideas on handling holidays when both work, as well as social concerns, were also discussed. Dealing with infidelity and its impact on the working couple was outlined, as well as dealing with sexual harassment both from the point of view of the couple as well as the individual who may need to make a complaint.

7

Have you got a problem? Your most common questions answered

This last section of the book is aimed at answering the most common problems that career couples encounter. My experience of working with career couples in counselling has introduced me to many of the kinds of questions that men and women ask about managing and balancing home and work life. The questions are grouped in sections that correspond to the chapters in this book. This is to help you look for more detailed advice and support in the appropriate section of the book. Each question and answer examines a specific difficulty, and although it may not be identical to your concern, you should be able to identify with some of the issues described in the questions.

Balancing home and work life

Q

Deidre, 29

I have just spent three years looking after our first child and am thinking about returning to work. I was a classroom assistant before I left and my husband is a fireman. What's the best way to make a decision? We could do with some extra money, but we can manage for a short while on my husband's wages.

A

You need to weigh up what you will gain or lose by returning to work. Think about the impact of work on your relationship with your husband and child, finances, social life and any other relevant issues. It could help to make a list under the various headings of 'fors' and 'againsts' to give you as wide a picture as possible of your choices. If you do decide to return to work, go to the school you worked for previously (always supposing you were happy there) to see if they have any classroom assistant posts available. Even if they do not have any vacancies, you might ask if they would be willing to give a reference for any work you wish to undertake in the future. If you are considering a career change, your local Job Centre may have information about career choice agencies in your area.

Q

Rowena, 34

My parents had a very traditional marriage. My dad worked on the railways and my mum looked after my three brothers and sisters and me until we left home. I am finding it hard to adjust to the idea that I will carry on working once my husband Michael and I start a family. Michael says that we can't afford for me to stop work completely, but I want to be a stay-at-home mum. How can we resolve our differences?

A

When one partner makes an assumption about another it can often cause problems. You come from a family who gave you a traditional way of thinking about family life, while Michael seems to have come from a family who had more liberal or independent views. You may be able to find a compromise to your differences by exploring a different way of working. For instance, your firm may be happy for you to work from home some of the time or to cut your working hours once you are pregnant. It could also help to look closely at your financial situation, making financial projections on your joint income in the next few years. You may both realise that you could manage for a longer time than the usual maternity leave would give, enabling you to take a longer career break of up to five years.

Q

Renu, 25

I am an Asian woman who has recently married. Although I am very happy in my marriage, my husband is not happy about me working. He feels that it is his role to support me. I want to continue working as a shop manager. I have done well in my job and was promoted at a young age. I would be sad to leave. How can I convince him I want to stay?

A

Your husband may have cultural reasons for wanting you to leave work – perhaps his background and family upbringing has pre-disposed him to believe that women should not work. Try talking to his family to find out if this is his personal belief or something that is shared by his wider family. If his objection is cultural or religious it could be useful to find out how other women in his family work and how they stayed in work. If his belief is a personal one – perhaps because he wants to protect and care for you – tell him how you feel. Be understanding, explaining how flattered you are that he wants to treat you so kindly, but also how much work means to you. You could also find it helpful to enlist the support of your own family who, presumably, have had no objection to you working.

Q

Adrian, 45

My partner and I have worked in offices all our lives and now feel ready to change careers. I have always been interested in woodwork and would like to set up a small business making furniture. My partner, Susan, is an amateur painter and would like to use part of the premises for a studio. But I am secretly worried that this will be too much togetherness. Might we argue more because of being together twenty-four hours a day?

A

It is possible that you will find being together all day is a big change in your relationship. The best way to tackle this is to talk through your concerns. Keeping them a secret means that neither of you can contribute to dealing with any potential difficulties as they emerge. You should also discuss ways of breaking up your days in a shared environment so that there are natural breaks when you are able to relax or spend some time apart from one another. You might find it useful to stagger working times, or screen off your working areas from each other, in order to allow for a little privacy.

See Chapter One for more information on these topics.

Building your relationship when you both work

Q

Sophie, 24

My partner Tony and I have just moved in together after going out as a couple for seven months. We are happy together except for one thing. The hour after we both get home from work is hell! We bark at each other and moan about work. We can have quite serious rows, usually about housework or lack of leisure time together, as well. How can we prevent this problem?

A

For many working couples, the meeting point at the end of the day can also be a crunch point! You may both be tired after work and travelling, as well as switching off work and switching on to being a couple. Try to avoid assaulting each other with work concerns or who should have bought the supper. Instead, agree that you will each have twenty minutes to be alone. During this time, change your clothes, take a shower or simply rest. Then sit down and share some time together – perhaps having a cup of tea. This 'gently, gently' approach will enable you to re-enter home life without feeling stressed. To prevent rows about housework, and who has or hasn't done their share, draw up a programme that clearly defines what you will both intend to do during the week. If one of you cannot keep your promises, explain why rather than allow your partner to harbour resentment because a task has not been carried out. You might also use your time together after work to plan what you will do for the evening, whether it involves watching a video together or going to a club. Be understanding if your partner is tired or wants to relax, but do plan for fun as this can help your relationship to survive.

Q

Ian, 52

My partner and I have lived together for three years. We are both divorced with grown-up children. I have my own business as a building material supplier. My partner Joyce works at a local hospital as an administrator. We have always had a good sex life, but lately we seem to have stopped making love. Joyce has been under pressure at work because her hospital has been threatened with closure and I have been concerned about a drop in my business profits. Could these things be affecting our sex life?

A

There is no doubt that anxiety can dampen down sexual feelings. You are both experiencing worries about your work and this could be diminishing your libido. You can raise sexual desire by ensuring that you make time to relax and forget about work concerns, even if only for a short time. You might also consider renewing some romantic memories – share a romantic meal, give a candlelit massage to each other or allow yourself the luxury of a shared breakfast in bed and a cuddle at the weekend. You could also talk through your mutual concerns about work. It's not uncommon for couples to seek to protect their partner from their worries, but this can mean that the burden of concern becomes very heavy and adversely affects the individual's response to the relationship, including their sex life. If you find that these simple measures do not help your sex life, consider seeking the help of a psychosexual therapist (see Further help at the back of the book).

Q
Kirsten, 40
My partner Terry and I want to move in together but cannot decide how to make this happen. Terry works from home as a freelance computer web site designer, while I travel to an office nearby. Terry does not want to move from his flat as he feels that it will mean a great deal of upheaval to let all his contacts know his new address. I want to stay in my house as I have recently put a lot of effort into decorating it. Should I move in with Terry or should he move in with me? We are now beginning to fight over this issue and it is spoiling an otherwise happy partnership.

A
It may be possible that neither of you is quite ready to set up together because you both clearly want to hold on to your independence in the shape of your individual homes. But you might solve the problem by choosing a completely new place for you both to live in. This will still mean that Terry has to alert all his contacts to the change, but it would be *your* shared place, as opposed to a take-over by one or other of you. If this is really out of the question, you could move into one or other of your homes and completely redecorate it in a different way. Give yourself time to decide whether you are really ready to share, as this seems to be the bedrock problem. It could be that you will feel clearer in a few months' time and more ready to move in together.

See Chapter Two for more information on these topics.

Managing your life together as a career couple

Q
Kathy, 37
My husband Julian and I want very different things from the next five years. I want to push my career forward because I am doing well at the moment. Julian wants to downshift, taking a reduction in salary so that he can work for a charity. I am not completely opposed to this, but could he come to resent my better earning power and work status?

A
Twenty-five years ago the strong expectation was that men would work in high-powered jobs while women would take jobs that did not compete with men. With the advent of the year 2000, all this has changed. Women can expect to have prestigious jobs and earn as much as their male counterparts. If Julian wants to take a different kind of job, perhaps one that is more satisfying, then your career should not come into the equation. As long as you offer him the same kind of support and respect for his role as he offers you for yours, there are no reasons why the relationship should be problematic. In fact, you could benefit from working in very different environments. Each of you can offer the other a different perspective on work issues that could enrich your approach to your jobs. Ensure that you spend time talking and discussing your feelings about work and you will avoid any potential difficulties.

Q
Irene, 55
My husband Lucas and I jointly run a small newsagent shop. We often run into problems, and have done for years, when tackling the ordering of goods. I like to take my time, looking at what has and hasn't sold. Lucas likes to order on impulse, often choosing things that do not do well in this area. We have never resolved this problem,

and I sometimes feel frustrated that Lucas refuses to listen to me. Is there a way round this after all this time?

A

You have obviously tussled with this issue for several years so it may be a question of accepting that you have very different approaches to the same concern. But you could get round it by suggesting to Lucas that he take charge of a different area to you. For instance, he may have the kind of quick mind that is creative and would be good at dressing the window. Alternatively, Lucas might research other stock items such as magazines or confectionery. Dividing the tasks into your personal preferences can be a solution when two people approach the same issue from different standpoints. You may have to weigh up whether the change you would like is worth the disturbance to the relationship. For instance, Lucas may regard it as a criticism or you may feel uncomfortable at initiating a change. Whatever the outcome, you may be able to manage the situation with patience over time.

Q

Neville, 30

I have always assumed that my partner, Gemma, would want the same kind of lifestyle as me. Now I discover that Gemma wants to live abroad while I intend my working future to be in this country. She is forever pushing applications for jobs in America at me and practically demanding that I look into living overseas. I do not want this. Can we survive these differences?

A

Gemma clearly has her own agenda about the future and seems to want you to fit into it, come what may. You need to explain, firmly and calmly, what you want to do, making it clear to Gemma that you are unlikely to change your mind. This may well spell the end of the relationship, but you are already on widely diverging paths and it may be that Gemma would eventually become frustrated that you will not join her in her desire to work abroad, and leave. It is always sad when a relationship finishes, but this may be the best way forward for the two of you when you have such differing expectations of the future.

See Chapter Three for more information on these topics.

The career couple and children

Q

Lucinda, 29

My partner and I want to have a child, but are not sure how to time the arrival of a baby. I am just about to take on some new responsibilities in my role as a PA and my partner is in a secure post in a bank. I intend to return to work after maternity leave, but how could this affect my career?

A

Although the decision to have a child is never easy, making a judgment about when to have a child in the context of your career can be complicated. In your case, you need to talk to your partner about the future and think through any commitments or changes that may be on the horizon. You mention 'new responsibilities' in your job. These may mean that you should get used to these before you decide to try for a baby. You could also talk in confidence to your personnel manager about your career prospects and how these may be affected by having a child. Take into account any drop in salary as well as any forthcoming promotional prospects. Check out childcare arrangements at your place of work or calculate the cost of childcare. Taking this kind of action can help you both to assess the impact of a child on you, your relationship and your careers. Once you have the full information you will feel more confident about the future.

Q

Bernard, 38

My wife Sindy and I have two small sons. My wife works full time while I have a part-time post at the local library. I have taken on the majority of the care of our sons, but this still doesn't seem to please Sindy. She complains that I don't do the washing and cooking to her satisfaction and that, because she works full time and I don't, she should do less in the home. I don't mind doing my share, but I resent being saddled with all the housework. How can we overcome this?

A

It feels as if you are being asked to sign up to a contract without reading the small print! Sindy obviously has assumptions about work and housework that you need to help her understand may not be realistic. Book time together to talk about this issue and explain what you are experiencing. Once you have made your feelings known, negotiate a more shared regime that allows free time for you as well as Sindy. It may be that Sindy is feeling overloaded at work but has not communicated this to you. Ask her about her workload and suggest that she speaks to her line manager if she feels she has to bear too much of a burden at work. Ensure that you have time together as a family and make time to be together just as a couple.

Q

Jason, 33

Since our baby son was born seven months ago we have not had an unbroken night's sleep. I find I cannot concentrate at work because I am so tired and my wife, Stephanie, is also exhausted. Is there any way we can cope with this? I am worried I may make a serious mistake one day.

A

This is an extremely common problem for new parents. Work and broken nights do not match and can eventually lead to relationship problems because you feel too tired to do anything but work and sleep (when you can). Your baby has taken a long time to settle into a routine so it may be time to consult a professional. I strongly suggest you seek the help of your local Health Visitor through your GP surgery; they will be able to help you with suggestions on encouraging your baby to sleep at night. In the meantime, keep up a regular bedtime routine with your baby and avoid taking him out of the cot once you have settled him down at night. This may be hard at first, but it can make a real difference after a few weeks.

See Chapter Four for more information on these topics.

The career couple and sex

Q

Melvin, 35

My girlfriend and I have a good sex life except that I feel really jealous of her work colleague, Matthew. I know he flirts with her because I have seen him do it at the firm's Christmas party. When we make love I keep thinking that she would rather be with Matthew. Should I confront her or not?

A

There really isn't very much to 'confront' your girlfriend with. Rather, you need to confront yourself and your jealousy. It seems as if your feelings stem from a low sense of self-esteem and that you cannot believe that your girlfriend likes you more than Matthew. It might help you to talk this through with your girlfriend, but ultimately you need to tackle the deep-seated emotions that you are experiencing. Counselling (see Further help at the back of the book) might help you to make sense of your jealousy.

Q

Miranda, 43

I work hard in my job as a deputy head teacher and often return home feeling tired. If my husband, Gary, asks me to make love when I am feeling tired, and I say no, he responds by saying I don't care about him and don't fancy him anymore. This is not true. When I am relaxed our sex life is great. How can I help him to understand my response?

A

Tiredness can certainly kill sexual feelings, but you might be able to explain to your husband how you feel in the following way. Explain that you are not rejecting *him*, but just the *act* of love-making on one particular night. Offer another time when you know you will be less tired, and stick to your promise. You might also suggest different ways to relax together to switch off from work – from a cosy supper together on a winter evening to a summer evening's walk in the local park – in fact, anything to let go of work and improve your relationship.

Q

Freya, 23

My boyfriend suffers from premature ejaculation and seems worse after he has been away on business trips. We have tried a number of ways to stop him ejaculating too quickly, such as thinking of something unsexy, but to no avail. Can he improve?

A

Yes, he can! The reason he is worse after a business trip is that his increased desire will make the premature ejaculation more pronounced. You could get round this by making love several times in a row. Usually the premature ejaculation is slowed by this technique. Alternatively, you could arouse your boyfriend to the point of ejaculation and then stop. Eventually this will help him to recognise the moment when he is about to ejaculate and he will be able to hold back. A psychosexual therapist can also help with this concern (see Further help at the back of this book).

See Chapter Five for more information on these topics.

Career couples and common problems

Q

Natasha, 36

My partner, James, works in a law firm that often asks its employees to socialise after work. James doesn't have to go, but fears that he may be viewed as uncommitted to the firm if he fails to accompany his colleagues to the club they frequent. Our relationship is beginning to suffer as he is often not home before 10 p.m. and as I have to leave for my job early in the morning, I am often in bed at this time.

A

This is not an easy problem to solve. Some firms do regard socialising as part of the 'deal' when working, but James may be able to draw a line some evenings. He could decide to go alternate evenings rather than every evening. It is possible that other people feel the same as he does and he could talk over the issue with a trusted colleague. Alternatively, you might agree to tolerate the situation for a further few months, but agree to reduce socialising once James feels more certain of his position in the firm.

Q

Barry, 50

Our holidays are always the same. My wife wants to lie on the beach all day while I want to try the resort's sports facilities. I only have a limited amount of holiday and would like my wife at least to take an interest in what I am doing or join me in swimming or snorkelling occasionally. Sometimes I feel we only meet up at the airport on the way home!

A

I wonder why she is reluctant to join you? Perhaps she feels you want her to take part in your choice of recreation but are unwilling to join her in her choice. Negotiate on this issue by offering to spend a day on the beach with her if she will spend a day with you. A little give and take could rescue your holiday and help you to feel more than strangers on the shore!

Q

Nerys, 38
Five weeks ago I discovered that my husband Clive was having an affair with a work colleague. I feel devastated and completely at sea. Clive has promised to give up the affair, but he will see the woman every day anyway. How can we recover from this terrible blow to our marriage?

A

Affairs can be very hard to handle and will require you to be honest about your hopes and expectations for the future. You both need to sit down and talk about what should happen now and try to unravel why the affair happened in the first place. Clive could investigate transferring to another department or location, because you may find his daily contact with his ex-lover too much to bear. Gradually you will recover your relationship and feel able to make decisions about the future, but this will take time and a lot of hard work before either of you can recover your equilibrium.

See Chapter Six for more information on these topics.

Afterword

The aim of this book has been to help couples who deal every day with the problems and pleasures of balancing home and work life. Each couple who works and tries to manage a relationship faces concerns unique to them that require ingenuity and creativity to solve. Many couples know that they succeed some of the time and struggle at other times.

The different subjects covered in this book are the most common issues that career couples have told me about during my counselling career. I have tried to pass on the learning that these real-life couples acquired as a result of talking about their concerns in the counselling room. Many of the exercises and other ideas have been tried by real couples who told me how valuable they found them and suggested other ways of working on similar concerns. I hope you also found them useful as an aid to working on your relationship.

Practical issues – such as arranging childcare – are also included in the book because if these go wrong or break down they can have a detrimental effect on a couple's relationship. For example, worrying about your child's carer while you are at work or blaming a partner for choosing the wrong carer can be avoided by following some of the guidelines in the book.

You may have found that you can adapt the ideas to fit your own circumstances. If this means that the book has provided an impetus to develop and improve your working relationship, it has served the purpose for which it was intended. I hope that it really has shown you how to *make love work for you* and will allow you to have a balanced relationship, with work, love, life and happiness all in the right proportions.

I wish you a successful working relationship in the future.

Further help

Counselling and similar agencies

British Association for Counselling
1 Regent Place
Rugby
CV21 2PJ
Internet: www.bac.co.uk
Tel: Helpline (information only) 01788 578328

This agency can provide lists of counsellors in your area for a wide range of issues, including unemployment, alcoholism, drug abuse, relationships, bereavement, AIDS/HIV, counselling in the health service and education. Contact the helpline for more information.

British Association for Sexual and Relationship Therapy
PO Box 13686
London
SW20 9ZH
e-mail: info@basmt.org.uk

This organisation holds lists of counsellors and therapists who specialise in couple and sexual therapy. To obtain listings or further information contact the address or e-mail above.

Cruse Bereavement Care
Cruse House
126 Sheen Road
Richmond
Surrey
TW9 1UR
Bereavement Line: 020 8332 7227

This organisation specialises in providing counselling for bereavement or issues associated with bereavement. Contact them on the helpline listed above.

British Association of Psychotherapists
37 Mapesbury Road
London
NW2 4HJ
Tel: 020 8452 9823

This organisation is the accreditation body for UK-based psychotherapy. Contact the number above for further information on psychotherapy or finding a psychotherapist in your area.

fpa (Family Planning Association)
2–12 Pentonville Road
London
N1 9FP
Helpline: 020 7837 5432

This group provides counselling and advice on sexual matters all over the country. They now also provide a 'Sexware' catalogue that includes sex aids that can be ordered by post. Contact the above number for further information.

MIND (National Association for Mental Health)
Granta House
15–19 Broadway
London
E15 4BQ
Helpline: Mind Info-line: 020 8522 1728 or 0345 660 163

MIND has over 200 centres offering help and support for anyone with concerns about their own or others' mental health problems. Contact them on the number above.

Relate
Herbert Gray College
Little Church St
Rugby
CV21 3AP
Tel: 01788 573241
Internet: www.relate.org.uk

Relate is the largest couple counselling and psychosexual therapy service agency in the UK. It has over 120 centres that offer counselling and psychosexual therapy to the public. Find your local centre in Yellow Pages or on the web site listed above.

Money and other financial concerns

National Debt Line
Birmingham Settlement
318 Summer Lane
Birmingham
West Midlands
B19 3RL

Helpline: 0645 500 511

This organisation gives advice to help people combat mortgage and rent arrears and other debts. Call the helpline for assistance in these matters (available only in the UK). A self-help information pack is also available.

Money Management Council
62 Manor Way
Beckenham
Kent
BR3 3LJ
Tel: 020 8658 8974

This agency can provide help in managing family financial issues. Contact on the number listed above.

National Association of Citizens Advice Bureaux
Myddleton House
115–123 Pentonville Road
London
N1 9LZ
Tel: 020 7833 2181
Internet: www.nacab.org.uk

The Citizens Advice Bureaux can provide free, confidential and impartial advice on any subject, but specialise in financial advice, particularly on debt problems. They have over 1000 offices in the UK. For further information contact them on the number and internet details above.

Parenting, pregnancy and childcare

Maternity Alliance
45 Beech Street
London
EC2P 2LX
Tel: 020 7588 8583

Maternity Alliance gives advice on the legal rights of parents, parents-to-be and mothers and fathers in the first year of their child's life. Contact their helpline on the listed number.

Home-Start UK
2 Salisbury Road
Leicester
LE1 7QR
Helpline: 0116 2339955

Home-Start schemes help parents of children under five who feel under pressure. They offer befriending and support, friendship and practical help to parents and children in their own homes. Contact on the number above.

Parentline UK
3rd Floor
Chapel House
18 Hatton Place
London
EC1N 8RU
Freephone helpline: 0808 8002222

Parentline provides support and help by telephone to anyone concerned about a childcare issue, especially where a parent feels under pressure. Call on the number listed above.

National Childminding Association
8 Masons Hill
Bromley
BR2 9EY
Tel: 020 8464 6164

Provides an information service on child-minding. Contact on the number above.

Contacts on legal matters

Solicitors Family Law Association
PO Box 302
Orpington
Kent
BR6 8QX
Tel: 01689 850227
Internet: www.ssla.org.uk/

Solicitors in this network specialise in family-related matters and in a conciliatory and constructive approach to family problems. Contact on the number listed above.

Law Centres Federation
Duchess House
18–19 Warren Street
London
W1P 5DB
Tel: 020 7387 8570

This organisation provides information about local law centres. Contact on the number listed above.

Index

advice
  counselling 133, 187–9
  financial agencies 189–90
  from friends or family 42
  legal 169, 192
affairs
  at work 28, 159, 184
  and the career couple 159–65
  coping after 162–5
  and mid-life crisis 27–8
  preventing 160–2
affection 46, 94, 130–1
age, and deciding when to have a baby 83, 87, 89
ageing 26–30
alcohol 122, 158
ambitions, and relationships 32–5, 177
anger 60, 112, 163
attitudes
  to the future 37, 178
  to parenthood 93–4
  to pregnancy 90–1, 92
au pairs 97–8

baby
  buying for the new 95–6
  deciding when to have a 86–9, 179
  effect on finances 94–6
  wrong reasons to have a 88–9
baby-sitters 102
bereavement 112, 160, 161

birth
  men supporting partner during 5, 92–3
  mother's age for first child 83, 89
  preparing for the 92–3
  returning to work after 90, 95, 172
  sex life after 120
  and your relationship 93–4, 160, 180
births outside marriage 6
body, improving self-confidence about your 126–8
breathing exercises 121
budgeting 43–5
business relationships, and couple relationships 61, 149–51, 155–6, 174, 177–8

career
  how will it fit into a new relationship 32–5
  and self-esteem 79–80
  stage in and decision to have a baby 83, 87
career couples
  and affairs 159–65
  answering common problems 171–84
  deciding whether to start a family 19–22, 83, 179
  during pregnancy 90–6
  and growing family 24–6
  issues mid-term 77–81
  life stages for 16–30
  maintaining successful relationships 54–81, 177–9
  in a new age 2–8
  problem busting 141–70

change, coping with 64–6, 69–71
child-minders 96, 99
childcare
    advisory agencies 191–2
    arrangements 96–100, 146–9
    cost of 20, 87–8
    discussing and planning 22–3
    history of 4, 5
    on holiday 157
    options 97–100
childlessness, choosing 19, 83, 86
children 82–110
    age gaps between 24
    coping with small 22–4
    deciding when to have 86–9, 179
    deciding whether to have 19–22, 83–9
    effect of arrival on your sex life 25, 101,
        113
    from a previous relationship 73–4
    how many to have 87
co-habiting 4, 6
    and financial effects of a new baby 94–5
    rights in 42, 95
    see also living together
colleagues
    and an office romance 166–8
    attitudes to your pregnancy 90–1
commitment
    effect on sex life 116
    and having a baby 88–9
communication skills 52–3, 56–8, 61, 82
contraception 83, 133
counselling agencies 187–9
couple relationships
    and business relationships 61, 149–51,
        155–6, 174, 177–8
    change in views of 4–5
creativity 86, 122, 142, 185
crèches 100
cultural differences, and beliefs about role of
    partner 7–8, 173

day nurseries 100
debt 38
decision-making, negotiation and 59–67
desire
    imbalance of 120, 139–40
    loss of 131–3, 135–6
    reawakening 132–3
    ups and downs in 114–15
diet 108, 121–2, 128
disagreeing
    as a habit 68–9
    publicly 68
discussion
    about money and sex 51
    of future plans in retirement 29–30
    reaching stalemate in 67–71
divorce 1, 22, 88
domestic work see housework
downshifting 142, 177
dreams 36, 122

drugs 122, 134
dyspareunia 136–7

emotional involvement, imbalance in 44
empathy 170
employers, and parents' rights 90, 95
erection, problems in achieving an 134–6
ethnic background, and beliefs about role of
    partner 7–8
exercise 120–1, 128
expectations
    about holidays 154–5
    about parenthood 84–6
    of partnerships 7, 32–5, 47
    sex role 79
eye contact 52, 125

family
    change in concept of 5–6
    deciding whether to have a 83–9
    thinking about starting a 19–22, 84–6
family budgeting 43–5
family life
    juggling work and 82–110, 142–9
    time together 102–3
    and working from home 152–4
father
    attending the birth 92–3
    involvement in childcare 146–9
    role during pregnancy 91–2
feelings, sharing 52–3
feminism 3
fertility rate 83
finances
    advisory agencies 189–90
    and deciding to have a baby 87–8
    and lifestyle 37
    and new parenthood 94–6
    problems 43–5
    in retirement 28, 29
    when you work together 150–1
friends
    seeking approval of 14–15
    your partner's 49

gay couples 6
gender differences, in approaching problems
    71–7
goals
    list of short, medium and long-term 32–4, 51
    shared 64–5
guilt 60, 107–10, 163

holidays 103, 154–8, 183
    when you work together 151
home
    setting up see moving in together
    working from 151–4
home/work balance 1–30, 51, 172–4
honesty 34, 61, 65, 79, 109, 162, 166
housework
    changes through history in views of 2–3, 5

difficulties 46–8
employing help 144–5
and living together 18–19
preference listing 143–4
strategies for managing 47–8, 143–6, 180

illness 112, 120, 132, 134, 148, 160
income, differences in 78–9
infidelity see affairs
intercourse, alternatives to 119–20
intuition 16, 120

jealousy 49, 88, 163, 168, 181
professional 78–80

legal advice 169, 192
libido, factors affecting 131–3, 158, 175
lifestyle 142, 178
busy and sex 115–16
and working mothers 23, 107–10
listening 61, 68, 125–6
living together
and housework 18–19
making the decision 18–19, 50–3, 174–6
love-making
planning for 114–15
practical help for 128–31
and relaxation 120–2

marriage 4, 6, 172
second or later 38–9, 87
maternity leave 87, 90, 93
men
as breadwinners 4
as fathers-to-be 91–2
'new men' 5
and problem-solving style 72, 74–5
problems in achieving an erection 134–6
and sex 46
menopause 133
menstrual disturbances 133
mid-life crisis 26–8
mistakes, learning from 43–9
money see finances
mothers, working 23, 107–10
moving in together
coping with 50–3, 174–5
deciding about 42, 176

nannies 98
negotiation
about socialising 49
financial 44–5
over housework 46–8
successful 45, 59–67, 73–4
NHS Patients' Charter 90

office affairs 159, 184
office romances 166–8

parenthood 82–110
assumptions about 84–6, 108

and employment rights 87, 90, 91, 95
making the decision 19–22, 84–6
small children 22–4
teenagers 25–6
toddlers 101–3
parenting agencies 191–2
parents
balancing their needs and yours 24, 39
elderly who may need care 88
partner
finding what he/she really thinks and feels
31, 52–3, 60, 64, 76, 115
helping you choose a 32–5
support for your 34, 75, 76–7, 168–9
partnerships see relationships
paternity leave 90, 91
pensions 28
planning ahead 41–2
pregnancy
advisory agencies 191–2
attitudes of colleagues to your 90–1
career couples during 90–6
role of the father during 91–2
unexpected 20, 43
working conditions during 90–2
premature ejaculation 182
problem solving 40–2, 61–2, 67–71, 141–70
problems
answers to common questions 171–84
differences in the way men and women see
71–7
potential 38–43
promotion
of one partner 78–9
and possible motherhood 20
psychosexual therapy 133, 134, 135

relationships
after the birth of a child 22, 88–9, 93–4, 113
and ambitions 32–5, 177
assumptions about 6–8, 18, 149, 178
building when you both work 31–53, 174–6
early on talking about your 35–8
effects of past 38–9, 43, 68–9
influence of other people on your 23, 80
maintaining successful working 54–81
making adjustments in 39–43, 58–67
MOTs for 55–8
moving from a casual into a long-term
17–18, 32–5, 50–3
new 35–8
potential problems 38–43
repairing after an affair 162–5
taking for granted 48, 77–8
talking about the future of your 51–3
varieties of 6
what do you want from? 32–5
what is your style? 8–16
see also career couples
relatives
caring for elderly 112
helping with childcare 98–9, 148

seeking approval of 14–15
relaxation 102–3
  and love-making 120–2, 135
religious background, and beliefs about role of
    partner 7–8
responsibilities
  in caring for baby 97
  changing 4–5
  parental when you both work 146–9, 180
  for teenage children 104–5
retirement 28–30
  early 28
role swapping 85–6
romance
  new 35–8
  in the office 166–8
routines
  breaking 16
  for children/toddlers 101–2, 142, 147–8
  developing by default 18
  for housework 48, 81, 145–6

sadness 60, 112, 163
school routines 147–8
self-awareness 8
self-employment
  and having children 93, 95, 107
  moving from employed work to 66
self-esteem
  and career 79–80, 142
  effect of an affair on 159, 161
  and having a baby 3, 88–9
  and loss of desire 131–2
  of teenagers 104–5
  your body image and 126–8
sex
  common myths about 113–16
  competitive 138
  differences in viewpoints between men and
    women 46
  frequency of 113–14
  initiating 139–40
  painful for women 136–8
  performance anxiety in men 134–5
  prioritising 117–18
  using as a weapon 68, 139
  see also love-making
sex life
  after children 25, 101, 113
  improving your 116–28
  lack of 115–16, 175
  and preventing affairs 161–2
  problems 45–6, 131–40, 182
  reasons for problems 112–13

talking about your 123–6
  and teenage children 105–6
  when you both work 111–40, 181–2
sexual harassment, coping with 168–70
socialising
  difficulties 48–9, 183
  patterns from before 80
spending 44–5
stress
  at work 34
  in the family 103, 104
  and sex 120, 131, 139
style
  background influences on 8–16
  learning about your partner's 23–4, 74–7

taking for granted 48, 77–8
teamwork 42–3, 48, 77, 103, 146
teenagers, coping with 25–6, 104–6
thrush 136
time
  for each other 45–6, 49, 78, 117–18
  for enjoying family life 102–3
  management 54, 80–1, 108
  not enough 47, 141–2
tiredness 19, 24–5, 180
  and sex 45, 101, 112, 131, 136, 139, 181–2
toddlers, coping with 101–3
trust 67, 71, 77, 101
  finances and 43–4
  lack of 112, 133, 159, 160
  rebuilding 165

undermining your partner 68

vaginismus 137

women
  changing roles of 2–4
  painful sex 136–8
  and problem-solving style 72–3, 75–7
  and sex 46
work 82–110
  history of relationships and 2–8
  importance in your life 32–4, 36–7
  later life and relationships 28–30
  managing social issues at 166–70
  mid-life change of patterns 26–7
  moving from employed to self-employed 66
  returning to after childbirth 90, 95, 147,
    172
  see also home/work balance
working from home 151–4
working together 149–51, 155–6, 174, 177–8